Speed Reading

The Ultimate Guide to Master Fast Reading

(A Simple Guide to Increase Your Reading Speed and Understanding)

Michael Corey

Published By **Phil Dawson**

Michael Corey

All Rights Reserved

Speed Reading: The Ultimate Guide to Master Fast Reading (A Simple Guide to Increase Your Reading Speed and Understanding)

ISBN 978-1-7770663-3-8

No part of this guidebook shall be reproduced in any form without permission in writing from the publisher except in the case of brief quotations embodied in critical articles or reviews.

Legal & Disclaimer

The information contained in this book is not designed to replace or take the place of any form of medicine or professional medical advice. The information in this book has been provided for educational & entertainment purposes only.

The information contained in this book has been compiled from sources deemed reliable, and it is accurate to the best of the Author's knowledge; however, the Author cannot guarantee its accuracy and validity and cannot be held liable for any errors or omissions. Changes are periodically made to this book. You must consult your doctor or get professional medical advice before using any of the suggested remedies, techniques, or information in this book.

Upon using the information contained in this book, you agree to hold harmless the Author from and against any damages, costs, and expenses, including any legal fees potentially resulting from the application of any of the information provided by this guide. This disclaimer applies to any damages or injury caused by the use and application, whether directly or indirectly, of any advice or information presented, whether for breach of contract, tort, negligence, personal injury, criminal intent, or under any other cause of action.

You agree to accept all risks of using the information presented inside this book. You need to consult a professional medical practitioner in order to ensure you are both able and healthy enough to participate in this program.

Table Of Contents

Chapter 1: Setting The Stage For Success. 1

Chapter 2: Techniques For Improved Comprehension 12

Chapter 3: Enhancing Memory And Retention 33

Chapter 4: Overcoming Barriers To Learning 51

Chapter 5: Advanced Speed Learning Strategies 63

Chapter 6: Studying? 77

Chapter 7: What It Is And How It Can Help You 84

Chapter 1: Setting The Stage For Success

Identifying your getting to know reason

Identifying your studying dreams is an vital first step in any gaining knowledge of manner. By absolutely defining your desires, you could make certain which you are focusing your efforts on the right topics and making the maximum of a while and assets. In this article, we will find out the process of identifying reading dreams and provide a few hints for placing effective getting to know goals.

The first step in figuring out your analyzing goals is to reflect to your contemporary-day talents and data. What do you understand and what regions do you experience you want to enhance upon? Are there specific competencies or facts areas which you want on your approach or career? Are there non-public hobbies or pastimes which you would like to research more about?

Once you have a elegant idea of the areas you would like to recognition on, it's far important to outline your dreams greater specially. Instead of simply putting forward that you want to "beautify your writing abilities," try and be extra particular via setting a intention which consist of "write a research paper using APA fashion quotation in the next six months." By putting a selected and plausible motive, you'll be able to tune your development and diploma your fulfillment greater effortlessly.

It is likewise vital to preserve in thoughts the time and sources to be had to you while setting your getting to know goals. While it may be tempting to set huge, bold dreams, it is crucial to be practical about what you could accomplish given your cutting-edge instances. Consider elements which incorporates your modern-day workload, any personal or family commitments, and any financial constraints you can have.

Once you have got recognized your mastering dreams, it's far important to create a plan for carrying out them. This need to include a timeline for completing your desires, in addition to any important steps or property. For example, in case your purpose is to look at a cutting-edge programming language, you may want to set apart specific times each week for reading, buy a textbook or on-line course, or find out a teach or take a look at enterprise business enterprise.

To developing a plan, it is able to be useful to enlist the help of others in undertaking your mastering dreams. This may additionally moreover need to embody finding a have a observe associate or turning into a member of a take a look at organisation, enlisting the assist of a mentor or teach, or truely sharing your goals with pals and circle of relatives for obligation and encouragement.

As you determine closer to attaining your mastering dreams, it's far important to music your development and make any vital changes to your plan. You can also find out that you want to alter your timeline or belongings as you skip, or that you need to set new goals as you development.

Overall, identifying your analyzing desires is an critical first step in any gaining knowledge of manner. By reflecting on your present day abilities and knowledge, placing particular and attainable desires, developing a plan, and enlisting the aid of others, you can set your self up for success as you parent inside the route of enhancing your capabilities and knowledge. So, it's miles always a top notch idea to spend a while figuring out your gaining knowledge of goals before starting any new mastering or development activity.

Creating a conducive learning surroundings

Creating a conducive reading environment is crucial for the success of any instructional organization, whether it's miles a college, university, or university. A high nice and supportive learning surroundings ought to have a massive effect on university college college students' motivation, engagement, and preferred preferred universal performance.

One of the most important elements in growing a conducive gaining knowledge of environment is the bodily setting. The school room or mastering place should be comfortable, nicely-lit, and well-ventilated. It ought to moreover be organized in a manner that promotes analyzing, with tables and chairs organized in a way that encourages interplay and collaboration.

Another crucial factor of a conducive analyzing environment is the usage of generation. In contemporary digital age, it's far vital for school rooms to have get proper of entry to to computers, capsules, and awesome digital gadgets. These gear can assist university college students get proper of entry to information, speak with their peers and teachers, and whole assignments.

To the physical setting and use of generation, the instructor performs a important function in growing a conducive analyzing surroundings. Teachers need to be supportive, approachable, and inclined to help college students who're struggling. They need to also be capable of create a nice and respectful observe room subculture, wherein all students revel in valued and protected.

Another key element of a conducive learning environment is the use of severa education techniques. Different college students analyze in unique techniques, and it's miles essential for instructors to use quite a few techniques to achieve all beginners. These strategies might consist of lectures, discussions, palms-on sports activities, and enterprise work.

Creating a excellent and supportive gaining knowledge of surroundings furthermore calls for the involvement of parents and guardians. They can play an crucial characteristic through the use of encouraging their youngsters to take part in splendor, setting apart a committed examine vicinity at home, and helping with homework and exceptional assignments.

It is important for faculties and academic institutions to provide assets and help for university children who may be suffering. This would possibly likely embody tutoring, counseling, or hotels for college children with studying versions.

Creating a conducive mastering environment is critical for the fulfillment of any academic agency. It requires a aggregate of a physical setting that is cushty and conducive to mastering, using technology, a supportive and approachable instructor, severa schooling strategies, decide and mother or father involvement, and resources and guide for suffering students. By prioritizing the ones elements, colleges and academic establishments can create a remarkable and supportive studying surroundings that promotes the success of all college students.

Time manage for inexperienced getting to know

Time manage is an crucial functionality for green gaining knowledge of, as it helps you to make the most of your have a test time and keep away from feeling overwhelmed thru your workload. Here are some guidelines for coping with a while correctly:

Create a time desk: One of the quality techniques to control it sluggish is to create a time table for your research. This can be as easy as a to-do listing for each day or a greater distinct plan that outlines what you need to have a study and whilst. Make positive to encompass breaks on your agenda to present your mind a relaxation and avoid burnout.

Set dreams: Setting dreams let you live targeted and inspired. Break your dreams down into smaller, greater practicable duties and deal with them one after the alternative. This will help you make development and enjoy a enjoy of achievement as you take a look at topics off your listing.

Avoid distractions: It's easy to get sidetracked on the same time as you are in search of to have a examine, so it's far crucial to limit distractions. Turn off your cellular telephone, discover a quiet area to art work, and limit your social media use. If you locate which you're without trouble distracted, consider using apps or software software that block distracting net web sites or assist you stay on course.

Take breaks: It's critical to take breaks while you're reading, as this may help you stay refreshed and targeted. Take a walk, perform a bit stretching, or chat with a friend to offer your thoughts a damage. Just make certain to agenda your breaks simply so they do not intervene together in conjunction with your studies.

Use some time correctly: Don't waste time on responsibilities that aren't important or that can be completed greater successfully. For instance, when you have to study an extended textbook bankruptcy, try skimming it first to get a experience of what is vital, then move lower lower back and focus at the information. This can help you store time and live focused on what's maximum essential.

Get prepared: Being organized let you store time and stay on track. Keep your test materials in a single region, take notes as you go, and use gear like flashcards that will help you evaluation and maintain facts.

Stay inspired: It may be hard to live brought on whilst you're going through pretty a few paintings, however it is important to discover methods to live advocated so you could make the maximum of a while. Set small rewards for your self as you complete obligations, discover a examine partner or be a part of a take a look at enterprise, and endure in mind to take care of your self with the aid of manner of having enough sleep and exercise.

By following those hints, you could make the maximum of your look at time and examine more successfully. Remember to be patient with yourself and do no longer get discouraged if you do not see results proper away. With time and exercising, you may get better at managing some time and analyzing more successfully.

Chapter 2: Techniques For Improved Comprehension

One way to do this is by using manner of previewing and browsing texts in advance than you've got a examine them in whole. In this text, we are able to discover what previewing and skimming are, how they can help you take a look at faster, and a few suggestions for correctly the use of those techniques.

What is Previewing?

Previewing is the approach of rapid searching over a textual content in advance than you examine it in full. It lets in you get a experience of what the textual content is about and what information it consists of. This may be specially useful when you have restricted time or are looking for particular information inner an extended text.

When previewing, you want to interest at the call, headings, and subheadings, in addition to any charts, graphs, or images which may be included. You can also look at the primary and ultimate paragraphs, as they regularly offer a precis of the primary elements of the text. By previewing the textual content, you can get a significant expertise of its content material and decide whether or no longer it's miles relevant to your needs.

What is Skimming?

Skimming is a reading technique that includes quick scanning a text to pick out its main factors and mind. It is similar to previewing, however it includes studying the textual content in more element. While previewing is centered on getting a famous expertise of the textual content, skimming is more centered on figuring out unique statistics or mind.

Skimming may be in particular useful even as you need to apprehend the number one factors of a textual content speedy, or whilst you are attempting to get a experience of the overall argument or shape of the text. When skimming, you need to cognizance on the first and final sentences of every paragraph, in addition to any bold or italicized phrases or phrases. These factors frequently include the primary mind or key elements of the text.

How Can Previewing and Skimming Help You Learn Faster?

There are numerous blessings to previewing and skimming texts while learning new facts. First, those techniques will let you keep time. If you are capable of preview or skim a textual content and decide that it is not relevant for your goals, you can keep your self the time and effort of reading it in complete.

Second, previewing and perusing will let you attention your analyzing. By getting a sense of the number one factors or thoughts of a textual content in advance than you study it in entire, you can more efficaciously turn out to be aware of what is maximum important and relevant on your analyzing goals. This will permit you to better recognize and preserve the fabric.

Third, previewing and skimming can help you increase your crucial wondering skills. By actively looking for the number one elements and thoughts of a textual content, you are wearing out a shape of assessment and evaluation. This will will can help you make bigger your capacity to turn out to be aware about the important component arguments and thoughts in a text and to understand how they relate to each other.

Tips for Effectively Using Previewing and Skimming

Here are some pointers for successfully the usage of previewing and browsing whilst analyzing new material:

Practice: The greater you exercise previewing and skimming, the higher you becomes at it. Start by way of previewing and surfing shorter texts and often increase the period and complexity of the texts you figure with.

Take notes: As you preview or skim a text, take notes on what you're studying. This will can help you higher understand and bear in mind the number one elements of the text.

Use headings and subheadings: Headings and subheadings assist you to get a enjoy of the general form and organization of a textual content. Use them to manual your reading and help you pick out the principle factors of the textual content.

Don't get too bogged down

Asking questions and predicting outcomes

Asking questions is an important problem of gaining knowledge of, as it lets in to make easy and solidify understanding of a topic. However, virtually asking questions isn't sufficient for powerful reading. In order to rush up the learning device, it is also useful on the way to are waiting for results and test hypotheses.

One method for predicting effects and attempting out hypotheses is known as the "question-prediction-final outcomes" (QPO) technique. This includes first asking a question about a topic, then predicting the final results or solution, and in the long run verifying the prediction via further take a look at or experimentation.

For instance, let's say you're analyzing about photosynthesis in vegetation. You may additionally start with the resource of way of asking yourself the query, "What is wanted for photosynthesis to occur?" You need to then make a prediction that photosynthesis requires daylight hours and water. To test this prediction, you can study about the manner of photosynthesis and notice in case your prediction is supported by the use of the information you research. If your prediction is correct, you may circulate right away to the following challenge matter with a more potent information of the problem. If your prediction is wrong, you may pass returned and revise your understanding of the challenge based totally mostly on the present day records you've got found out.

In addition to helping you examine more efficiently, the QPO technique has severa other advantages. It encourages lively wondering and allows to foster critical wondering competencies. It additionally helps you to grow to be aware about any gaps on your statistics, so that you can popularity your gaining knowledge of at the regions in that you need the most improvement.

Another powerful method for predicting results is known as "scenario planning." This consists of imagining splendid viable destiny outcomes for a given state of affairs and considering the opportunity of every outcome taking region. This may be useful for making selections, because it helps you to anticipate the potential results of your actions.

For example, permit's recall you are attempting to determine whether or not or not to take a interest offer from a modern-day organization. You want to use situation planning to preserve in mind the capability results of accepting or rejecting the provide. You could possibly bear in thoughts factors which incorporates the enterprise's financial balance, the fantastic of the artwork environment, and the capability for career development. By weighing the experts and cons of every situation, you may make a more informed decision approximately whether or not or now not to simply accept the assignment provide.

In addition to being a beneficial tool for selection-making, situation planning also permit you to to check extra efficiently with the useful resource of forcing you to don't forget a couple of perspectives and effects. It encourages you to suppose creatively and to keep in mind the functionality results of your actions.

Asking questions and predicting effects are every essential skills for effective analyzing. By using strategies in conjunction with the QPO approach and situation making plans, you may boost up your studying and gain a deeper expertise of any hassle. Whether you're a student in search of to have a look at new fabric or an character looking for to decorate your statistics in a selected place, those techniques allow you to to research extra successfully and successfully.

Taking notes and summarizing

Taking notes and summarizing are crucial abilties a terrific way to will let you study extra effectively and correctly. When you're taking notes, you're actively enticing with the material and focusing your attention on the most critical facts. Summarizing permits you to condense that statistics into a extra potential shape, which could make it a great deal much less complex to examine and consider. In this newsletter, we are going to find out the benefits of taking notes and summarizing, and provide a few hints and strategies for doing them efficiently as a part of a velocity studying manner.

First, allow's bear in mind the advantages of taking notes. When you take notes, you're compelled to be aware about the material, instead of genuinely passively listening or reading. This lively engagement helps you to higher understand and don't forget the statistics. In addition, the act of writing down the statistics enables to enhance it in your memory. Research has tested that scholars who take notes carry out better on assessments than folks who do no longer, and that taking notes with the aid of hand is extra powerful than typing them on a laptop.

There are severa one-of-a-kind techniques to taking notes that you could try, depending to your personal learning fashion and the cloth you are going for walks with. The Cornell Method includes dividing your notes into 3 sections: a slender left-hand margin for key elements, a much broader proper-hand margin for elaboration, and a small segment at the bottom for a precis. The Outline Method involves developing a hierarchy of records, with important points at the pinnacle and assisting info under. The Mapping Method includes developing visual representations of the material, which includes thoughts maps or idea maps.

Once you've got taken your notes, the following step is to summarize the statistics. Summarizing lets in you to condense the cloth right right into a greater viable form, that can make it much less complicated to check and recollect. It also lets you choose out the important factor factors and maximum essential thoughts, it is essential for statistics and synthesizing the cloth.

There are numerous techniques you may use to summarize efficiently. One technique is to create a list of the primary elements or key mind. Another is to install writing a short precis of the fabric to your very own terms. This can be useful for expertise the cloth, in addition to for reviewing and remembering it later. You can also attempt developing visible summaries, in conjunction with thoughts maps or concept maps, which may be a useful way to prepare and represent the data.

In addition to taking notes and summarizing, there are numerous specific strategies so one can permit you to take a look at more successfully and successfully. These embody:

Reviewing your notes and summaries regularly: Reviewing the fabric you have located out is an critical part of the getting to know manner. By reviewing your notes and summaries often, you could assist to decorate the records in your memory and beautify your know-how of the fabric.

Asking questions: Asking questions can help you to make clear your expertise of the fabric and discover any regions that you want to check.

Teaching someone else: Teaching the fabric to someone else can be a powerful way to boost your knowledge and pick out any areas in which you want to check.

Practicing: Practicing what you've got were given located, through sports sports inclusive of fixing troubles or finishing exercising quizzes, assist you to to decorate your competencies and maintain the statistics.

In give up, taking notes and summarizing are vital abilties for inexperienced and powerful studying. By actively attractive with the fabric, condensing it right right into a extra viable form, and reviewing and operating in the direction of what you have got were given observed out, you may enhance your knowledge and retention of the cloth and observe extra effectively.

Using mnemonic devices

Mnemonic gadgets are a amazing manner to beautify your reminiscence and observe new matters quicker. These strategies use institutions and hints to help you don't forget statistics greater effortlessly, and can be particularly useful for memorizing big quantities of facts or for gaining information of latest capabilities.

One commonplace mnemonic tool is the usage of acronyms. An acronym is a phrase usual from the number one letters of a series of terms, at the side of NASA or HIV. Acronyms may be a useful manner to consider lists or sequences, as they invent a memorable word that you may with out issues recollect. For instance, in case you favored to don't forget the order of the planets within the solar tool, you can use the acronym "My Very Educated Mother

Just Served Us Nine Pizzas," with every letter representing a planet: Mercury, Venus, Earth, Mars, Jupiter, Saturn, Uranus, Neptune, and Pluto.

Another mnemonic device is the usage of rhymes or songs. Rhymes and songs are memorable because of the reality they are easy to undergo in thoughts and are regularly fun to use. For example, you can use a rhyme to keep in mind the colours of the rainbow: "Red, orange, yellow, inexperienced, blue, indigo, violet." You also can use a tune to do not forget the times of the week, which include "Sunday, Monday, Tuesday, Wednesday, Thursday, Friday, Saturday."

Visualization is any other powerful mnemonic tool. This approach includes developing a highbrow photo or affiliation with the statistics you want to recollect. For instance, in case you favored to go through in mind the names of the Great Lakes, you can visualize them as lakes on a map, or you may associate each lake with a selected image or object. This permit you to endure in mind the names of the lakes greater results.

Another mnemonic tool is the use of reminiscence palaces. A reminiscence palace is a highbrow location or place which you create for your mind, and you could use it to preserve and keep in mind data. To create a memory palace, you start via imagining a acquainted vicinity, which include your property or a place you have got were given visited in advance than. Then, you "area" the items you want to don't forget in unique places interior that region. For example, you might imagine a pink vehicle to your driveway to symbolize the phrase "purple," or a sofa for your residing room to symbolize the phrase "sofa." By associating the gadgets you want to remember with particular places to your reminiscence palace, you could greater without issues don't forget that statistics.

There are many one-of-a-kind mnemonic devices you could use to decorate your memory and mastering pace. For example, you may use the method of loci, which includes visualizing a course or adventure and placing the items you want to undergo in mind alongside that course. You also can use the pegword technique, which incorporates associating new facts with a list of acquainted words or gadgets that you already recognize well.

Using mnemonic gadgets can be a amusing and powerful manner to decorate your memory and observe new subjects quicker. Whether you operate acronyms, rhymes, visualization, reminiscence palaces, or each one of a kind mnemonic approach, those strategies will can help you bear in mind statistics more without problems and enhance your studying velocity. So next time you have got got to investigate some thing new, attempt using a mnemonic tool to help you keep the statistics extra efficaciously.

Testing and quizzing yourself

Self-checking out and quizzing are powerful gear that permit you to research and maintain new records more efficiently. When you check your self, you engage with the material in a deeper and more huge manner, which facilitates you higher apprehend and keep in mind what you've got observed. By quizzing your self regularly, you could moreover understand any gaps on your statistics and attention your observe efforts on the regions wherein you need the most improvement.

One of the key blessings of self-trying out is that it permits you actively approach the cloth you are gaining knowledge of. When you in truth look at or be aware of a lecture, an awful lot of the records you take in is passively absorbed. You may be capable of keep in mind some of it in some time, however the records is not completely included into your lengthy-term memory. On the opportunity hand, at the same time as you test yourself, you actively retrieve the facts out of your reminiscence, which enables to enhance the connections for your thoughts and make the fabric greater eternal.

Self-trying out can take many bureaucracy, collectively with traditional paper-and-pencil quizzes, flashcards, and on-line quizzes. The format you select will rely on your private getting to know fashion and the shape of material you are reading. For example, flashcards may be a first rate desire for studying vocabulary, even as a conventional quiz can be more suitable for trying out your expertise of complicated necessities.

It's important to observe that self-checking out is best even as it's far spaced out through the years. If you try to cram all your studying right proper right into a unmarried session the night time earlier than an exam, you can no longer be giving your self the opportunity to definitely system and keep the records. Instead, try to quiz yourself at everyday periods over an extended time body. This will allow you to gradually constructing up your expertise and provide your mind time to consolidate the new fabric.

Another powerful way to check your self is to attempt to offer an motive for the fabric to a person else. This may be in particular useful if you are having hassle expertise a concept. When you try to provide an motive behind some component to a person else, you are pressured to consider the cloth in a unique way, which can help you discover any regions of misunderstanding. You can also moreover moreover discover that the act of explaining the fabric to someone else allows to solidify your know-how of the idea.

In addition to self-finding out, there also are some of distinct strategies that will let you observe and maintain new statistics greater successfully. One of those is using mnemonic gadgets, which can be memory aids that assist you partner new data with a few component you recognize. For example, you may use the acronym "ROY G. BIV" to don't forget the colours of the rainbow (crimson, orange, yellow, inexperienced, blue, indigo, violet). Mnemonic gadgets can be a useful device for memorizing lists or sequences of information.

Chapter 3: Enhancing Memory And Retention

The significance of sleep and bodily video games.

Sleep and exercise are essential factors that may significantly effect your capability to research and keep records. In this newsletter, we are capable of find out the significance of sleep and workout for pace reading and the manner you could incorporate the ones conduct into your every day ordinary to beautify your cognitive overall performance.

First, allow's speak approximately sleep. It is at some point of sleep that our brains consolidate memories, process new data, and smooth out pollutants. Without ok sleep, our cognitive talents go through, main to decreased ability to pay interest, hold in mind new records, and make alternatives. In truth, studies has shown that individuals who get a excellent night time time's sleep are higher capable of test and keep new facts in evaluation to folks who are sleep deprived.

But how an awful lot sleep do you need to optimize your gaining knowledge of abilities? The National Sleep Foundation recommends 7-nine hours of sleep consistent with night time time for adults. This may additionally moreover additionally variety barely relying for your age, manner of life, and regular fitness, but the key is to aim for a consistent sleep time table and prioritize getting a whole night time time's rest.

In addition to the amount of sleep, the outstanding of sleep is also vital. A sleep environment this is too warm, too cold, or too noisy can disrupt your sleep and impact your cognitive overall performance. To enhance the excellent of your sleep, you may try the following:

Establish a bedtime ordinary: Creating a regular bedtime ordinary can help sign up your frame that it's time to wind down and prepare for sleep. This need to include sports activities in conjunction with studying, taking a warmth bath, or working towards relaxation techniques.

Avoid shows earlier than bed: The blue slight emitted with the aid of using manner of video display units can intervene with the producing of melatonin, a hormone that permits modify your sleep-wake cycle. To beautify your sleep, try to avoid video display devices for at the least an hour in advance than mattress.

Create a snug sleep environment: A cushty sleep surroundings is important for a superb night time time's rest. This consists of a comfortable mattress, a room that isn't too warm or bloodless, and a noise degree this is conducive to sleep.

In addition to sleep, ordinary exercising is also crucial for optimizing your cognitive standard performance. Exercise has been confirmed to beautify reminiscence, boom blood waft to the mind, and reduce the risk of cognitive decline. It also can help to reduce pressure and enhance your temper, both of which could have a effective impact on your functionality to investigate and preserve new records.

So how masses workout do you need to beautify your studying skills? The Centers for Disease Control and Prevention recommends at least 100 and fifty mins of moderate-depth exercising consistent with week for adults, or 75 minutes of energetic-intensity workout. This may be damaged down into shorter schooling in the course of the week, which includes a 30-minute stroll or workout each day.

But it's miles now not without a doubt the amount of workout that subjects – the form of exercise you do can also have an effect on your cognitive normal overall overall performance. Research has tested that sports activities sports that require coordination and balance, including dancing or yoga, can also have a specially powerful impact on thoughts feature.

Incorporating sleep and exercising into your every day ordinary may want to have a extensive impact for your capability to research and preserve new records. By prioritizing those habits, you can optimize your cognitive ordinary typical performance and enhance your regular fitness and nicely-being. So next time you are attempting to boost up your mastering, consider the significance of sleep and exercising.

Spaced repetition and interleaving

Spaced repetition and interleaving are evidence-based totally strategies that may help college students have a look at more effectively and successfully. In this newsletter, we are going to discover what these strategies are, how they artwork, and the way you can use them to hurry up your getting to know.

Spaced repetition is a studying technique that includes spacing out the periods amongst reviewing or working towards formerly located out fabric. The concept inside the lower back of this technique is that with the aid of the use of reviewing material at increasingly longer periods, you can enhance your memory of the material and decorate your retention of it over the years. There are several particular spaced repetition algorithms that you could use to decide the fine periods for assessment, however a commonplace approach is to observe cloth more regularly on the start and then frequently growth the intervals among evaluations as you grow to be more acquainted with the fabric.

One of the key benefits of spaced repetition is that it lets in you to check fabric in small, feasible chunks instead of in search of to take in a large amount of facts abruptly. This makes it less tough to cognizance on the fabric and decreases the chance of forgetting what you have located out. Additionally, due to the fact you're reviewing the material at ordinary durations, you can trap any gaps in your facts in advance than they turn out to be too difficult to repair.

Interleaving is some different technique that can help you observe more efficiently. This technique includes blending one-of-a-kind sorts of cloth or duties collectively in desire to that specialize in one issue at a time. For instance, if you're studying for a records examination, you may likely interleave your analyzing through manner of reviewing a passage on historical Rome, doing some math issues, after which reading a passage on medieval Europe.

The concept at the back of interleaving is that with the aid of constantly switching among high-quality types of material, you are forcing your thoughts to alternate among one in all a kind highbrow models. This allow you to live engaged and centered, and it may moreover assist you assemble connections between superb portions of records. Additionally, due to the fact you're continuously exposed to new material, you'll be more likely to keep what you are getting to know over the long term.

So, how can you operate those techniques to rush up your analyzing? Here are some tips:

Use spaced repetition software program software: There are some of apps and web sites that can help you agenda your critiques and exercising instructions the use of a spaced repetition set of rules. These equipment can be specially useful when you have an entire lot of material to test or when you have a tough time remembering at the same time as to have a study specific items.

Mix up your observe periods: Instead of specializing in one difficulty or mission at a time, try interleaving your studying via switching amongst wonderful subjects or duties. This can assist preserve you engaged and also can assist you gather connections among one-of-a-kind portions of records.

Take breaks and vary your have a take a look at vicinity: It's critical to offer your thoughts a break on occasion, especially if you're trying to take in hundreds of facts. Take regular breaks to stretch, take a walk, or do some detail else that you revel in. Additionally, try studying in particular places to maintain matters exciting and to help your thoughts make new associations with the material you're mastering.

Overall, spaced repetition and interleaving are effective strategies as a way to will let you studies more efficaciously and correctly. By spacing out your reviews and combining up your have a look at lessons, you may decorate your reminiscence, enhance your retention of latest material, and accelerate your reading.

Using memory palaces and specific visualization techniques

Memory palaces and distinctive visualization strategies may be effective tools for reinforcing your reading and do not forget of statistics. In this article, we're capable of discover what memory palaces are, how they paintings, and the manner you could use them and unique visualization techniques to hurry up your gaining knowledge of.

So, what exactly is a reminiscence palace? A memory palace is a intellectual illustration of a physical place which you're familiar with, which encompass your property or your college. To use a memory palace, you begin thru visualizing a particular vicinity to your mind, and then you definately without a doubt vicinity various portions of facts or "memory devices" for the duration of that location. For instance, you could region a memory item at the the front porch, every extraordinary in the residing room, and so on.

To consider the records later, you truely need to "walk through" your reminiscence palace and retrieve the reminiscence gadgets in the same order that you placed them. Because you are the usage of visualization and spatial memory to shop and retrieve the facts, this approach can be very powerful for analyzing and recalling complex or precis statistics.

Memory palaces are actually one instance of visualization techniques that may be used to enhance reading and consider. Other visualization strategies that you could use embody:

Mind maps: A mind map is a graphical illustration of statistics that indicates the relationships amongst first rate portions of data. To create a mind map, you start by manner of using writing the precept idea or concept in the center of the web net page and then draw strains to attach it to related thoughts or subtopics. Mind maps can be mainly useful for organizing and data complex information.

Concept maps: Similar to mind maps, idea maps display the relationships amongst precise standards or thoughts. To create a idea map, you start via writing the number one idea inside the middle of the web page and then draw strains to attach it to associated thoughts. Concept maps may be in particular beneficial for expertise the relationships between precise thoughts or for organizing and summarizing information.

Graphic organizers: Graphic organizers are visible equipment that assist you organize and recognize facts. There are many one-of-a-type kinds of photograph organizers, which encompass go along with the go with the flow charts, Venn diagrams, and tree diagrams. Graphic organizers can be specially useful for visible rookies or for organizing and understanding complicated data.

So, how can you use those visualization techniques to speed up your studying? Here are a few guidelines:

Create a memory palace: If you've got pretty some data to observe and preserve, preserve in thoughts creating a memory palace to help you arrange and keep in mind the cloth. Start with the useful resource of visualizing a physical region that you're familiar with and then location the information you need to consider in some unspecified time in the future of that region.

Use thoughts maps or idea maps: If you've got were given severa complicated facts to investigate, go through in mind developing a mind map or concept map to help you set up and recognize the relationships between high-quality portions of records.

Use photo organizers: If you are a seen learner or if you have pretty a few complex information to understand, remember the use of picture organizers that will help you installation and apprehend the material.

Overall, reminiscence palaces and exclusive visualization techniques may be effective tools for boosting your getting to know and remember of records. By the use of those strategies, you may put together and apprehend complex cloth more without difficulty, and you may be capable of boost up your gaining knowledge of as a quit result.

Applying what you examine thru practice and application

Learning new abilties and mind is an critical part of non-public and professional improvement, and one of the handiest techniques to do that is through workout and application. By actively utilizing what you have got located, you can't handiest beautify your understanding of the material, however additionally hold it for longer intervals of time. In this text, we are able to discover the blessings of practising and utilising what you observe, and provide some tips for incorporating these behavior into your learning regular.

One of the primary blessings of practice and application is that it helps you to higher understand and keep the material you are learning. When you absolutely look at or be aware of a lecture, the data can be resultseasily forgotten because it has no longer been actively processed with the aid of your thoughts. However, at the same time as you actively engage with the cloth thru workout and alertness, your thoughts is forced to assume significantly and make connections among the state-of-the-art information and what you understand. This enables to solidify the data on your reminiscence and make it much less complicated to keep in mind afterward.

Another benefit of practice and alertness is that it lets in you to emerge as aware about any areas of inclined component or misconception. When you're simply passively consuming statistics, it may be smooth to miss key standards or overlook approximately approximately regions that you don't virtually understand. However, even as you actively practice what you've got were given discovered out, you're much more likely to encounter roadblocks or areas of misunderstanding, which can then be addressed and clarified.

In addition to those cognitive blessings, working towards and utilizing what you have a look at also can assist to growth yourself guarantee and motivation. When you're capable of efficaciously exercising a contemporary functionality or concept, it can come up with a enjoy of success and encourage you to maintain analyzing. This can be in particular beneficial at the same time as tackling difficult fabric or topics that can to start with appear daunting.

So, how will you comprise exercising and alertness into your getting to know ordinary? Here are some pointers:

Find ways to actively interact with the fabric. This can embody taking notes, asking questions, or participating in discussions.

Practice troubles or bodily sports related to the material you are studying. This can be specially useful for subjects like math or era that require fingers-on application.

Create real-global examples or situations wherein you may examine the cloth you're gaining knowledge of. For instance, in case you are mastering about advertising and advertising and advertising, try to provide you with a hypothetical marketing marketing and marketing advertising and marketing marketing campaign and spot how the mind you are studying should exercising.

Seek out possibilities to use the capabilities or information you're studying in a realistic putting. For instance, if you are gaining knowledge of a brand new programming language, strive building a small project or contributing to an open-supply project.

Work with others to practice and practice what you are getting to know. Collaborating with others can help to deepen your information of the fabric and offer a brand new mind-set on how it could be achieved.

In give up, schooling and using what you look at is a critical part of the getting to know method. It allows to beautify your knowledge and retention of the material, understand areas of weak factor, and growth yourself belief and motivation. By actively looking for possibilities to interact with and apply the fabric you're learning, you can boost up your analyzing and higher prepare your self for fulfillment in your private and professional endeavors.

Chapter 4: Overcoming Barriers To Learning

Dealing with procrastination

Procrastination is a not unusual trouble that influences people of every age and walks of existence. It may be described because the act of delaying or postponing duties, regularly because of a loss of motivation or interest. While it could look like a innocent dependancy, procrastination can also have severe results on every our non-public and expert lives. It can bring about neglected final dates, decreased productivity, and advanced stress and anxiety. In the context of tempo mastering, procrastination may be especially detrimental, as it may prevent us from making the maximum of our look at time and accomplishing our whole capacity.

So, how are we able to correctly deal with procrastination and overcome this risky addiction? Here are some strategies that may be useful:

Identify the concept cause of your procrastination.

Before you can address your procrastination, it is critical to understand what is causing it. Are you feeling crushed thru the quantity of labor you want to do? Are you missing motivation or interest inside the project to hand? Or are you perhaps experiencing a few extraordinary personal trouble that is affecting your potential to popularity and get matters finished? By identifying the underlying purpose of your procrastination, you may better cope with the hassle and discover solutions on the way to give you the results you want.

Set clean desires and cut-off dates.

One of the number one reasons people procrastinate is due to the fact they do no longer have a easy experience of what they need to do or maybe as it wishes to be finished. Setting unique dreams and closing dates permit you to stay centered and encouraged, because it gives you a experience of motive and direction. When placing desires, make certain they will be possible, measurable, and applicable for your common targets. Deadlines, then again, want to be practical however no longer too a protracted way within the destiny.

Break duties into smaller chunks.

Large, complicated duties can be intimidating and overwhelming, that can result in procrastination. To make topics more possible, strive breaking your responsibilities into smaller, greater possible chunks. This will make it much less complicated to get began and preserve going, as you may reputation on one piece at a time alternatively of getting crushed thru the entire task.

Create a exquisite getting to know environment.

Your surroundings could have a large effect on your functionality to interest and live recommended. To create a effective studying environment, discover a quiet, comfortable area to artwork in which you won't be interrupted or distracted. Consider factors along side lights, temperature, and furnishings while choosing a test area. Also, attempt to eliminate as many distractions as possible, collectively with turning off your cellphone or final vain tabs for your pc.

Use productiveness gadget and strategies.

There are many machine and techniques so that it will permit you to live on the proper track and avoid procrastination. For instance, you can use a planner or to-do list to put together your duties and time table, or attempt the Pomodoro Technique, which includes operating in brief, targeted bursts placed through brief breaks. Other tools and strategies that can be useful encompass time blocking off, the Eisenhower Matrix, and the 50/10 rule.

Get obligation from others.

Accountability may be a powerful motivator, because it offers you someone to report to and maintains you responsible for your actions. You can get obligation from others in some of strategies, at the side of running with a study partner, becoming a member of a observe group, or hiring a teach or educate. By having a person to reply to, you will be much more likely to live on path and keep away from procrastination.

Take care of your self.

Procrastination can frequently be a sign of burnout or stress. To be your exquisite self and avoid falling into the procrastination trap, it's miles critical to take care of your self.

Managing tension and stress

Anxiety and stress may be number one barriers to reading. When we are traumatic or careworn, our brains are not inside the first-class kingdom for absorbing and retaining new statistics. It's crucial to control anxiety and stress that allows you to facilitate pace reading.

One effective manner to manipulate tension and stress is thru using relaxation strategies. These can embody deep respiration, modern-day muscle rest, or mindfulness meditation. Deep respiration involves taking gradual, deep breaths in through the nose and out through the mouth. This facilitates to lighten up the frame and calm the thoughts.

Progressive muscle rest includes tensing and enjoyable one-of-a-kind muscle companies in the frame, beginning with the toes and going for walks as a great deal as the top. This helps to launch anxiety and sell relaxation. Mindfulness meditation consists of focusing on the present 2nd and accepting thoughts and emotions without judgment. This can help to lessen strain and increase reputation.

Another manner to manipulate anxiety and stress is thru the use of tremendous questioning. This entails reframing negative mind and changing them with first-rate ones. For instance, in vicinity of questioning "I'll in no manner be able to examine this cloth," try wondering "I'm able to learning this cloth, and I'll art work at it until I understand it." This shift in attitude can help to lessen tension and boom motivation.

Exercise is each different powerful manner to manipulate tension and stress. Physical interest releases endorphins, which can be chemical materials within the mind that assist to beautify mood and decrease strain. Exercise also can help to lessen emotions of anxiety and improve popular properly-being.

It's also vital to manipulate time successfully even as looking for to analyze new fabric brief. This can include putting clean goals and breaking them down into smaller, greater possible duties. It can also contain prioritizing responsibilities and focusing on the maximum crucial ones first.

Another useful approach is to vary the manner wherein new records is observed out. This can include using incredible techniques which include reading, writing, talking, or listening. Varying the strategies of studying can assist to hold subjects exciting and make the material simpler to recognize.

It's additionally critical to take breaks while studying new cloth. Taking breaks lets in to save you burnout and lets in the mind to way and consolidate new information. It's a top notch concept to take brief breaks each hour or so and to time table longer breaks every few hours.

Finally, seeking out aid from others may be an effective manner to manipulate tension and stress. This can contain speaking to pals or family members, on the lookout for the manual of a counselor or therapist, or turning into a member of a assist enterprise. Receiving assist from others can help to reduce emotions of isolation and enhance sizeable well-being.

In conclusion, handling tension and strain is an vital issue of pace studying. Techniques collectively with rest, terrific wondering, exercise, powerful time manipulate, numerous learning techniques, and searching for help can all assist to lessen anxiety and strain and facilitate the mastering approach. By the use of those strategies, you can boom your capability to research new material speedy and effectively.

Coping with distractions and interruptions

Distractions and interruptions can be a great venture to getting to know, in particular at the same time as attempting to analyze some aspect fast. However, there are strategies to deal with these distractions and interruptions to be able to improve your speed learning.

One of the high-quality techniques to address distractions and interruptions is to lower them as heaps as viable. This can incorporate finding a quiet, isolated location to art work in which you could no longer be interrupted through others, turning off your cellphone or precise digital devices, and ultimate unnecessary tabs or windows for your computer. If you are working with a group, you can moreover try setting clean barriers and guidelines to decrease disruptions.

Another beneficial method is to workout mindfulness, which includes being gift within the second and focusing for your mind and movements. This assist you to live on course and keep away from getting sidetracked with the aid of manner of distractions. You can exercise mindfulness through taking a few deep breaths and focusing for your breath, or through the usage of a mantra or extraordinary mental cues to hold your self grounded.

It's additionally essential to be proactive in dealing with it sluggish. This can include placing easy dreams and priorities, breaking large obligations into smaller, more doable ones, and the usage of a planner or to-do list to stay prepared. By taking manage of a while and staying organized, you can lessen the opportunities of having sidetracked or interrupted.

One technique that can be specially effective for tempo studying is the Pomodoro Technique, which incorporates operating in targeted 25-minute increments accompanied by way of the usage of manner of brief breaks. This assist you to live targeted and avoid burnout, as well as offer you with the opportunity to take breaks and refocus your hobby at the same time as wished.

Another key element of coping with distractions and interruptions is gaining knowledge of to say no. It's critical as a way to set obstacles and prioritize your non-public studying and productivity. This can also suggest turning down invitations or requests for assist that could distract you from your analyzing goals.

It's also beneficial to domesticate a increase mindset, which includes viewing demanding conditions as possibilities for increase and analyzing, instead of as setbacks. This allow you to live prompted and resilient inside the face of distractions and interruptions, and might make it much less difficult to get higher and get lower lower back on course at the identical time as you do get sidetracked.

Chapter 5: Advanced Speed Learning Strategies

Using technology on your advantage

Technology has revolutionized the manner we research, presenting an entire lot of equipment and assets that might help us acquire new information and competencies at an progressed tempo. From on-line courses and video tutorials to academic apps and software application application, there are endless strategies to leverage technology to your gain at the identical time because it comes to hurry studying. In this article, we're going to find out some of the crucial issue strategies you can use technology to enhance your gaining knowledge of functionality and acquire your desires quicker.

One of the primary blessings of technology is that it permits us to get entry to a exceptional array of records and belongings from everywhere, at any time. With the net at our fingertips, we are able to find out solutions to simply any query, or have a look at any situation remember that pastimes us. This way that you can use era to observe a large form of topics, whether or not or not or not you're in search of to enhance your expert abilties, benefit a modern day hobby, or in reality expand your information.

Online publications and video tutorials are a famous desire for lots rookies, as they provide a based and available way to research new talents. There are endless internet sites and systems that provide courses on everything from programming and layout to corporation and personal development. Many of these courses are self-paced, so you can improvement at your personal pace and suit your analyzing spherical your different commitments.

In addition to online guides, there also are many educational apps and software program software application that can help you research new subjects faster. For example, there are language getting to know apps that use interactive video video games and sporting sports to help you select out up a brand new language speedy, and there also are academic apps for quite quite a number topics collectively with math, technological understanding, and history.

Another manner to apply generation to your gain is by using the use of it to create a customised analyzing enjoy. For instance, you may use mastering manipulate systems (LMS) to create custom learning paths, or use adaptive gaining knowledge of software program application that adjusts the content material cloth and problem stage based on your person dreams and development. This let you live added approximately and focused, as you're learning at a tempo it surely is right for you.

Technology can also help you examine extra efficaciously through providing device and belongings that guide exceptional analyzing patterns. For example, a few human beings have a look at superb with the useful aid of visual approach, while others opt to have a look at through hands-on sports or taking note of lectures. Technology can provide some of resources to manual the ones one-of-a-type studying styles, consisting of video lectures, interactive simulations, and virtual fact reviews.

Finally, generation let you analyze quicker with the aid of manner of supplying get proper of entry to to a worldwide network of novices. With social media, forums, and on-line businesses, you can connect with other novices and percent your stories, ask for recommendation, and get feedback for your development. This can offer valuable help and encouragement as you discern toward your analyzing goals.

In conclusion, technology gives some of device and resources that permit you to studies new topics faster. From online guides and educational apps to personalized studying and community help, there are infinite methods to leverage technology on your benefit. By the usage of these resources accurately, you can boost up your reading and attain your goals more rapid.

Forming take a look at companies and taking factor in collaborative learning

Collaborative studying is a technique of teaching and analyzing that includes college students running collectively in small businesses to solve problems, talk requirements, and proportion records. One manner to interact in collaborative learning is to form a have a examine institution. Study organizations can be an powerful manner to rush up the analyzing device and beautify performance on tests and assignments. In this text, we're going to discover the blessings of forming take a look at groups and taking element in collaborative studying, and provide some suggestions on a manner to create and participate in a achievement have a take a look at organizations.

One of the number one benefits of forming have a look at companies is that they allow college college students to percentage data and mind with every one of a type. When university college students work together, they are in a position to talk their first-rate perspectives on a subject and bring together on each particular's thoughts. This technique can assist university college college students to apprehend principles greater completely and preserve facts extra correctly. In addition, have a examine corporations can provide a experience of manual and motivation. When students are part of a hard and fast running inside the route of a not unusual cause, they may be much more likely to live heading inside the proper course and stay stimulated to research.

Another benefit of study companies is they can help college students to boom critical abilities together with communique, hassle-solving, and control. When college university college students are required to offer an motive behind their thoughts to their buddies and pay attention to the mind of others, they're capable of enhance their communique competencies. Similarly, operating collectively to clear up troubles and entire agency assignments can assist university college students to make bigger problem-solving skills. And, at the same time as students are given the possibility to guide company discussions or cope with different control roles in the have a have a have a look at agency, they might boom control competencies in case you want to be precious in their academic and expert careers.

So, how are you going to create and take part in a a success examine institution? Here are a few tips:

Start with the useful resource of locating a difficult and rapid of college students who are dedicated to reading and willing to location in the try to be triumphant. It's essential to select organisation individuals who are dependable and could show as lots as meetings and contribute to the organisation's discussions and sports.

Set clear goals and expectations for the corporation. Determine what you desire to accumulate through the take a look at group and the way you can degree your improvement. This will help to hold the business enterprise focused and ensure that everyone is jogging inside the direction of the equal dreams.

Create a time table and keep on with it. Establish a regular assembly time and vicinity that works for all group people. It's critical to be regular and display as masses as conferences on time as a way to make the most of your have a look at organization time.

Encourage participation from all corporation participants. Make sure that everyone has the possibility to make a contribution to the organization's discussions and sports activities activities. This can be mainly crucial for introverted or shy group people who won't talk up as frequently.

Use a number of gaining knowledge of strategies. Study businesses can be more powerful after they use a whole lot of analyzing strategies, which encompass communicate, trouble-fixing, and assessment video games. Mixing topics up can help to maintain the institution engaged and can also help to enhance terrific varieties of studying.

Stay prepared and hold authentic statistics. Keep track of the business enterprise's improvement and any vital notes or materials from conferences. This will let you live heading in the right route and make the most of your have a have a look at enterprise time.

In give up, forming have a observe groups and taking issue in collaborative studying can be an effective way to hurry up the reading manner and enhance general performance on checks and assignments. By sharing facts and thoughts, developing critical abilities, and staying prepared, college college students can create a success look at businesses that help them to accumulate their getting to know goals.

Incorporating multimedia and diverse reading techniques

Incorporating multimedia and special reading strategies can substantially beautify the rate and effectiveness of studying. By the use of quite some one in all a kind gaining knowledge of techniques, we are able to cater to the numerous learning wishes and options of individual beginners, and make the learning revel in greater engaging and fun.

Multimedia refers to using diverse media office work, consisting of text, photographs, audio, and video, within the technique of analyzing. Incorporating multimedia in studying can offer a more immersive and interactive learning enjoy, as well as assist inexperienced human beings higher understand and keep the fabric.

For example, in case you are analyzing a modern day language, you may use multimedia sources together with movies, podcasts, and interactive video video video games to exercising your listening and speaking competencies. Multimedia resources can also be used to demonstrate complex necessities and offer actual-lifestyles examples, that could make the mastering more big and relevant to beginners.

Diversified learning strategies, but, speak to the use of masses of unique strategies and procedures to getting to know. By incorporating a number of getting to know techniques, we will cater to the one-of-a-kind studying patterns and alternatives of person novices, and make the studying experience greater personalized and powerful.

For instance, in case you are a visible learner, you could gain from using techniques collectively with thoughts maps, diagrams, and charts to arrange and apprehend the fabric. If you're a kinesthetic learner, however, you may benefit from palms-on sports activities activities, collectively with experiments or simulations, to have interaction with the cloth in a more interactive way.

Incorporating each multimedia and varied mastering strategies can also moreover have a number of blessings for speed studying. By imparting green persons with severa particular studying experiences, we will hold them engaged and stimulated to observe. This can help to reduce the time it takes to investigate the material, as newcomers are more likely to maintain the information and be capable of check it in a big manner.

Furthermore, thru catering to the various reading goals and alternatives of person newbies, we are capable of create a more inclusive and powerful gaining knowledge of environment. This can assist to reduce frustration and decorate newcomers' self guarantee and self-esteem, that can in turn enhance their motivation to investigate.

There are many wonderful tactics to encompass multimedia and one-of-a-kind learning strategies within the analyzing technique. Some of the only strategies encompass:

Using multimedia belongings together with movies, podcasts, and interactive games to illustrate complicated necessities and provide real-life examples.

Creating mind maps, diagrams, and charts to visualize and prepare the fabric.

Engaging in palms-on activities, together with experiments or simulations, to exercise and exercise the cloth in a extra interactive way.

Providing novices with quite a number diverse mastering substances, which include books, articles, and on line sources, to cater to their various learning desires and picks.

Encouraging beginners to artwork in corporations or pairs, as this can provide a greater collaborative and interactive learning revel in.

Incorporating multimedia and varied getting to know techniques can substantially decorate the fee and effectiveness of studying. By catering to the numerous getting to know dreams and alternatives of individual beginners, and offering them with some of numerous learning reviews, we can create a more engaging and exciting mastering environment that enables inexperienced folks to hold the material and follow it in a great manner.

Chapter 6: Studying?

Are you prepared to revolutionize your method to studying and optimize your overall performance? This ebook gives the requirements to understand pace studying, acquire your studying desires, and, most importantly, apprehend the critical points at the same time as staying prompted. Before we dive into this thrilling topic, permit me percent my journey with you.

I actually have constantly had a difficult time taking part in studying. This grow to be a source of problem for me at some point of my research, as I wanted assist studying and revising my publications well. However, I had to attain my research, so I attempted to have a look at as speedy as feasible to assimilate the expertise I end up lacking. Unfortunately, my efforts were in useless, and I could not understand what I became reading.

When I become trying to overview philosophy education, I couldn't follow the authors' complex reasoning and maintain the records. Similarly, once I needed to have a look at a unique in French, I determined it dull and couldn't get into the story.

After many months of research, I in the long run understood my hassle: I could not recognize the texts I end up reading, and my analyzing speed grow to be under average. That's once I determined the speed-studying method. I observed out that I could not most effective apprehend better but additionally faster. So I spent my time mastering a manner to have a have a look at efficiently and the way the eyes art work, and subsequently, I completed 1/three in my class.

Today, my purpose is to proportion my revel in thru a e-book. I preference involved humans can discover pace analyzing techniques from the start of their studies, simply so they don't should waste months seeking out them like I did. This will keep them time and cause them to more a fulfillment of their research.

For instance, way to tempo analyzing, I have to have a take a look at philosophy books in half of the time and apprehend them better. Similarly, I must study French novels with greater pleasure and maintain the tale's info higher. I am confident that the ones strategies will gain definitely anyone, and I preference my ebook can help many students decorate their studying and comprehension of texts. It saves time and allows them beautify their studies at the identical time as playing studying more.

Since I positioned the velocity-analyzing approach and placed the suggestions I decided out into workout, I discovered that many human beings round me additionally had issues with studying. So, I decided to proportion my statistics with them and became overjoyed to locate it useful.

I met a co-employee who needed assist analyzing and information commands for a venture. I suggested him to practice the fee-reading techniques I had found out, and after a few weeks of exercising, he advised me that it made a large distinction for him. He need to examine and understand instructions heaps faster, which helped him be greater organized and get the task finished.

I additionally met a friend who changed into making geared up for an exam and desired help studying and preserving facts. I recommended her to exercise tempo reading strategies, and she or he or he knowledgeable me it changed into useful. She may additionally want to study and recognize the texts she had to research a whole lot quicker and surpassed her examination with flying sun shades.

These examples display the importance of learning and discovering strategies to apprehend facts better. Speed reading is a on hand approach that would assist humans enhance their mastering and success, no matter their place of interest or purpose. That is why it can advantage absolutely everyone, and I desire my e book can help many college college students and experts decorate their studying and comprehension of texts. I need my e-book to be a deliver of motivation for anybody who wants to beautify their analyzing and achievement, and reading can be a treasured tool in accomplishing this intention.

This e-book is supposed to teach you to speed reading techniques and tips for reinforcing your comprehension and do not forget of texts. However, it's miles important to be conscious that pace reading is a way that requires exercise and training to be completed effectively. So, without a doubt as a ebook on swimming on my own isn't enough to understand the way to swim, the same is real for this e book and tempo studying. To improve your studying and comprehension, operating in the direction of the suggestions and strategies on this ebook with the critical issue requirements in thoughts is vital.

It's critical to understand that you'll want extra than just studying books about tempo studying to beautify. The real key to achievement in our business enterprise is chronic, dedicated workout. You have to make the effort to study this e book greater than once, now not truly as fast as. By doing so, you could make sure which you absolutely realize the strategies and advice supplied and that you can use them to your advantage each day.

Regarding speed studying, the adage "workout makes perfect" couldn't be more relevant. You need to actively positioned the techniques into practice each time you've got the hazard in place of simply reading approximately them. Take benefit of each risk to workout your newfound talents, whether or not or now not studying a bankruptcy in a ebook, a bit of writing within the newspaper, or perhaps a brief electronic mail. The more you use the techniques, the extra snug and natural they'll experience, resulting in proper advancement and improvement.

The secret to accomplishing your pace reading objectives is consistency. Do your excellent to consist of the strategies into your ordinary sports and hold going proper now if you word any adjustments. Even even though the versions might not be obvious right now, they in the end grow to be smooth. You'll have a study greater brief and be able to have a look at and understand substances more speedy and effectively.

Chapter 7: What It Is And How It Can Help You

Have you ever idea about how plenty time you spend analyzing every day? Reading emails, on-line articles, books, and reports for work also can moreover soak up a whole lot time, and in advance than you apprehend it, your complete day has surpassed. But don't forget what you could do with all that point in case you invested it efficiently. Imagine being capable of study extra rapid, efficaciously, and comprehensively. It ought to have a big effect on each your private and professional life.

It is plain what advantages quick studying has. You can boom your records and maintain awareness of a huge form of subjects through using the usage of analyzing extra rapid and through extra material in a whole lot a good deal much less time. This may be specially useful in a professional setting in which you want to examine and realise reviews and place of work paintings unexpectedly. Gaining performance and productivity thru speedy reading will located you in advance of the competition.

Consider all the novels you've longed to study but have by no means decided the time. Think about how many more you can observe if you could check them greater speedy and with higher comprehension. Reading must be a tool for gaining knowledge of and development in desire to idle time. You can turn each minute you spend reading right right into a worthwhile funding in your self in case you examine the expertise of speedy reading.

Refrain from allowing time to stand in the way of your achievement and development. It's as a incredible deal as you to make the maximum of every minute thinking about all of them rely. You can store time, boom your information, and create new possibilities for increase and improvement thru speed reading. So don't wait; get started out proper away to your route to a faster, extra compelling reading.

Fortunately, there's a studying approach that permits you to do just that: pace studying. Speed analyzing will assist you to examine quicker while preserving a excellent expertise of what you're analyzing. This approach you may have a have a look at greater in a lot much less time while expertise what you're studying better. It's a valuable potential that assist you to reap all elements of your lifestyles, whether it's artwork, school, or non-public life.

Speed studying is a way that allows you to take a look at quicker even as preserving a excellent expertise of what you are studying. This way you may read more in lots much less time at the same time as facts what you're reading better. This approach is available and permit you to shop time, apprehend the texts you have got a have a look at better, and don't forget them extra with out problem.

Imagine how masses time you could keep every day if you check faster. You need to look at in-intensity articles in much less time, apprehend your boss's emails higher, or maybe stop your excursion books extra rapid. And that's not all! Speed analyzing moreover permits you higher apprehend the text you test, which means that that which you'll be able to keep the information better and use it more successfully. Thanks to the fee-analyzing technique, you'll also be capable of don't forget it more effortlessly.

The origins of pace analyzing circulate decrease lower back many centuries. As early as antiquity, Greek philosophers which consist of Plato and Aristotle advanced speed analyzing strategies to recognize better and maintain their friends' writings. Since then, the price-studying approach has been perfected over the centuries.

During the eighteenth century, many thinkers and educators started out out to interest on pace analyzing and to study its effects on learning and comprehension. One of the primary to without a doubt popularize the rate-analyzing approach changed into the French author and fact seeker Voltaire, who used tempo reading to rapid take a look at and apprehend massive quantities of textual content.

In the twentieth century, tempo reading became more and more famous manner to educators which include Evelyn Wood and Tony Buzan. Wood advanced a pace-studying method based totally mostly on eye motion and key-phrase popularity. At the identical time, Buzan popularized velocity analyzing through using memorization and visualization techniques to assist people look at faster and higher understand what they've a look at.

Speed analyzing is a way that has been advanced and perfected over the centuries, however it has end up typical in contemporary years. But why? What has introduced approximately this extended popularity of speed studying in recent years?

There are numerous motives why tempo reading has emerge as so famous in current years. First, we stay in a global wherein statistics is anywhere. We are constantly bombarded with emails, articles, notifications, and messages. To maintain up, we need techniques to study faster and better understand what we're reading. Speed reading allows us to do really that.

In addition, tempo reading has turn out to be famous in current years because of the truth it may be utilized in hundreds of one among a type contexts. Whether you are a scholar, a professional, or honestly someone who loves to look at, tempo reading will will let you acquire your goals faster and further effectively. It assist you to research greater speedy, apprehend what you look at, and keep in mind it greater outcomes.

Finally, tempo analyzing has come to be famous in modern-day years way to the numerous equipment and property available for individuals who need to analyze this talent. Whether you select out books, movies, or on line publications, there are masses of procedures to take a look at pace analyzing and become a pro.

But how does pace studying paintings? And how can you use it to decorate your every day life? This ebook will discover the basics of tempo studying and display how this technique allow you to acquire your dreams. We'll have a take a look at a manner to use pace analyzing to research quicker, remedy problems greater efficaciously, and make higher picks more speedy.

Speed studying is a precious capacity in an effort to permit you to reach all elements of your lifestyles. So, organized to discover the secrets of pace reading and grow to be a studying pro? Let's get commenced out!

III. What are the capabilities required to understand tempo analyzing?

Mastering tempo analyzing requires precise tendencies and capabilities that can be evolved and progressed over time. Here are a number of the important functions to need to understand speed reading:

Motivation: Mastering pace reading takes time and effort, so it is important to have strong motivation and clean desires. If you have got a excellent cause to decorate your reading, you will be much more likely to exercising the strategies and persevere even because it turns into difficult.

Concentration: Speed reading calls for popularity and awareness at the textual content for prolonged periods. If you have were given problem concentrating or paying interest, it is crucial in advance than reading to rush look at.

Skimming: Skimming includes no longer studying each word in isolation however skimming the textual content to get the gist. To try this, you want with a view to examine diagonally and short find out key phrases and critical data.

The potential to device information fast: Mastering tempo reading moreover includes processing information quick and setting it into perspective to recognize its this means that. If you've got were given problem processing facts fast, it's far vital to art work on this capability earlier than you start getting to know to hurry read.

Mental Flexibility: Finally, studying pace studying requires intellectual flexibility and the capability to conform fast to new situations. If you have got were given hassle adjusting to new conditions or converting your thinking, running on this capacity in advance than you start studying tempo analyzing is critical.

Mastering velocity reading requires sturdy motivation, the capacity to pay interest, take a look at diagonally, tool facts short, and feature highbrow flexibility. If you work on those developments and abilties, you'll be able to grasp pace analyzing and experience all of the advantages it can deliver on your learning and success. Remember, it's miles important and exercising often to decorate those skills and acquire your speed-studying dreams.

There are many techniques and techniques for enhancing the ones functions and capabilities, and you could find out many suggestions and sporting occasions on this ebook to help you boom them. Take the time to take a look at and workout the ones hints, and don't hesitate to exercising regularly to peer real improvement for your analyzing and comprehension. With motivation, attention, skimming capacity, highbrow flexibility, and the capability to method statistics quick, you can draw close velocity reading and benefit your pace-reading dreams.

Everyone can learn how to read speedy irrespective of age, training stage, or line of exertions. It's a preferred misperception that human beings with precise abilties or skills are the only ones who can look at quick. But now not something can be further from the fact than this. Anyone may also additionally moreover studies and decorate their velocity analyzing abilities with commitment and attempt.

The inclinations and skills needed for instant analyzing, which consist of reputation, skimming, and quick facts processing, want to be cited that they'll be now not situations. Don't surrender, even in case you remember you presently lack particular abilities. Through training and exercise, they may be honed and advanced. Therefore, rapid reading is available to all of us, whether or not or not or no longer they want to keep time on their studying duties as university college students, end up more efficient as experts, or studies greater.

It is plain what blessings short studying has. You might also hold time, studies extra, and be extra productive thru the use of analyzing extra speedy and with higher comprehension. Your non-public and expert lives is probably substantially suffering from this. You can enhance your academic overall performance or expert opportunities and loose up extra time by means of using figuring out your complete analyzing potential.

You need so that it will advantage your full ability as a reader with out worry or inexperience. Anyone inclined to put effort and time can discover ways to test speedy. So take fee of your reading right now and set off on your course to becoming a quicker, extra effective reader. Your funding in time and knowledge can be greater than worthwhile.

IV. Three prerequisites to beautify your knowledge

Understanding the connection between analyzing pace and understanding is important. Even although those competencies are cautiously associated, they may be nonetheless various things that can be discovered independently. For readers to emerge as effective, it's miles critical to understand this difference.

Both studying comprehension and pace are essential abilties that may notably have an impact in your non-public and professional life. You can also have a bonus for your training or work if you could swiftly and effectively acquire and understand information. However, reading fast doesn't always mean which you fully apprehend the ebook. On the alternative hand, reading slowly even as genuinely knowledge the cloth might be time-eating and require extra time to assimilate massive quantities of information efficaciously.

It is critical to pay attention on both analyzing comprehension and velocity. Faster reading with better comprehension can prevent you from overlooking essential statistics or misinterpreting the material. It's crucial to balance speed and know-how due to this. You may additionally moreover enhance your studying overall performance and capability to realise information by using way of using jogging on every capabilities simultaneously.

It's additionally important to bear in mind that those talents can be received over the years thru education and exercise. Therefore, hold in thoughts that it's typically feasible to get higher in case you want assist with every velocity or comprehension. You may additionally decorate your analyzing tempo and overall performance to understand information greater rapid and effectively with dedication and strive.

Pay interest to every capabilities and artwork to boom analyzing comprehension and pace. By operating on each, you could maximize your reading skills and benefit a bonus to your university or career. Therefore, try and exercise always, and you will acquire the rewards of analyzing in a well-rounded manner.

Before we circulate at once to the following chapters on velocity studying techniques, it's miles critical to attention on 3 conditions that might appreciably growth studying tempo and comprehension of texts.

First, lexical poverty may want to have massive most vital importance to hurry reading. Indeed, if you don't recognize the which means of fantastic terms, you'll be compelled to slow down your analyzing to recognize them or to save you completely to look for their definition. This can down your studying pace and adjust your know-how of the text. Working on your vocabulary to have a look at fast and really recognize the texts you're reading is crucial.

Second, studying slowly can clearly impact your comprehension. If you study too slowly, you could have problem following the argument's drift and remembering data inside the textual content. By growing your studying pace, you can gadget more facts in an lousy lot much less time, allowing you to understand better what you observe.

Finally, a lack of hobby or motivation also can effect your knowledge of texts. If you aren't interested by the issue you are studying about, you can have a tendency to lose attention and bypass over important statistics. Similarly, in case you don't have the incentive to investigate or understand the text, you'll be lots less probably to make the effort to have a look at it cautiously and memorize it. Finding topics you're captivated with and developing your motivation for studying to maximise your comprehension of the texts is critical.

Lexical poverty

Reading comprehension is a vital skills that lets in you to have a look at and understand statistics. However, there are times while you may need help expertise a text, even if you have an incredible studying tempo. In some times, those comprehension troubles can be due to lexical poverty, i.E., a lack of vocabulary.

Here's how lexical poverty might also have an impact in your text comprehension:

1. You may additionally additionally moreover want assist expertise the that means of terms: You want to realise the importance of a phrase to understand the significance of the textual content as a whole.

2. You can also have problem following the writer's argument: If you need assist

information the writer's phrases, you can check their reasoning and recognize their mind.

3. You also can need assist remembering the content material of the text: If you want assist information the which means of terms, you may want help putting the content material of the text.

Vocabulary is an critical a part of our language and our potential to speak. The more phrases you have got were given at your disposal, the extra as it should be and expressively you may percentage. However, every so often you can want help finding the proper words, or you could need to examine the meaning of powerful terms. Fortunately, there are many ways to strengthen your vocabulary and end up a better communicator. Here are some smooth steps to comply with:

1. Read often: Reading is a superb way to study new phrases and support your

vocabulary. Choose books that hobby you and undertaking you to find out phrases.

2. Do vocabulary bodily games: many sporting occasions and video games permit you to look at and maintain new terms.

three. Use a dictionary: If you don't comprehend the which means of a word, appearance it up in a dictionary. This will help you understand the phrases' importance and the textual content better.

four. Talk with humans: Talk with those who use a rich and diverse vocabulary. This will assist you find out new phrases and better understand their use.

5. Write often: Writing is every one-of-a-kind great way to apply vocabulary. Try to use new terms in your writing and look for new processes to mention matters.

You can significantly decorate your reading comprehension via constructing your vocabulary and working closer to analyzing often. Remember, reading comprehension is a potential discovered over time and with exercising, so maintain operating and enhancing.

Insufficient studying tempo

Your capability to apprehend and recollect records from a text can be extensively impacted with the useful useful resource of the rate you examine. It can only be easy to recognize the general relevance and which means of the textual content you are reading if you examine slowly. This might likely make it extra difficult to apprehend the argument and apprehend the important information and connections the various thoughts, making analyzing plenty less satisfying.

Slow studying must have a dangerous effect on comprehension further to inflicting boredom, aggravation, and a lack of preference to test extra. These unfavorable feelings must make it tougher a good way to pay attention and realise the text, making it greater tough to do not forget what you are reading. Furthermore, studying slowly ought to make you greater confused because of the reality you may sense compelled to maintain up with folks who look at quicker or surrender fabric through way of a specific remaining date.

On the opportunity hand, studying at a tempo that lets in you to maintain your interest at the text and recognize its content can enhance your comprehension and reminiscence. You can more genuinely look at the argument, apprehend the number one elements, and apprehend the connections among requirements at the same time as you take a look at at a cushty pace. By doing so, you can discover reading greater interesting and be higher able to consider what you take a look at.

It's important to don't forget that reading comprehension and velocity are remarkable capabilities that may be superior one after the alternative. While reading unexpectedly may be performed with out always records the whole lot examine, analyzing slowly additionally may be done at the same time as statistics the e-book absolutely. These talents work together to create a well-rounded studying approach that permits you to check fast while but knowledge the textual content altogether.

It's crucial to workout regularly if you need to boom your analyzing comprehension and pace. This can entail workout exercises to sharpen your focus and focus and techniques like skimming, scanning, and previewing. To keep away from weariness, which can also obstruct your studying capability, it's also important to take breaks, stretch, and rest your eyes.

Compelling reading is based upon on each analyzing speed and comprehension. Working on your comprehension talents will permit you to make sure which you completely don't forget the material you examine, although it's critical to take a look at at a tempo that allows you to focus and realize the which means of the text. You can turn out to be a extra effective and green reader by means of manner of using locating a balance among those talents and regularly running closer to, in an effort that will help you test quicker, more really, and extra fun.

It is essential to be aware that the proper reading pace varies from man or woman to character and depends on many elements, which include the person's comprehension stage, the form of textual content, and the purpose of the studying. However, analyzing too slowly can typically result in comprehension and memory problems. Reading too short can cause troubles because of desiring extra time to method and take into account statistics.

Increasing your studying tempo permits you to approach more facts in less time and better understand and keep what you look at. Reading quicker, you can maintain near the text's wellknown because of this and understand the author's argument higher. You also can be capable of hold crucial statistics from them greater with out troubles because of the fact your brain may also have time to memorize it as you've got a examine on.

Lack of hobby or motivation

We need to underline how crucial it's far to understand that extended analyzing comprehension can not be received by myself via the usage of growing studying pace. One must bear in mind different factors to beautify your capability to understand and hold knowledge.

The effectiveness of your studying skills is greatly prompted thru greater factors, along side preserving a immoderate degree of focus and recognition. Your brain methods and maintains facts greater efficiently while completely engrossed in what you're studying. Because of this, it's miles essential to hold your interest inside the hassle and your motivation immoderate.

Interest inside the trouble can considerably effect your ability to apprehend and go through in thoughts statistics. Your mind is much more likely to actively interact with the content material while you are analyzing some factor you are captivated with, which results in a deeper degree of mastering and do not forget.

Although reading speed plays a extensive feature in information, it is not the quality. To sincerely enhance your studying capabilities, it's miles important to endure in thoughts additional factors which includes degree of reputation, pressure, and exuberance for the difficulty.

For instance, if you aren't centered on what you're reading, you will have problem retaining information and knowledge the text. Similarly, if you don't have motivation or hobby within the task rely, you'll be much less probable to have a look at cautiously and take the time to apprehend vital data.

Working on your focus and motivation to maximise your comprehension of texts is essential. You can, as an instance, discover a quiet, distraction-loose environment to observe in, set easy and motivating reading dreams, or find out topics you are passionate about to encourage you to read.

V. Eye functioning in analyzing

The fovea, placed in the middle of the macula, is the vicinity of the retina wherein visible acuity is maximum acute because of the presence of varieties of photoreceptor cells in this place: cones and rods. The cones, commonly touchy to coloration and detail, are handiest in colourful mild. In comparison, the rods, which can be specially touchy to solar sunglasses of grey and motion, are in particular beneficial inside the dark or at night time.

It is critical to word that cones constitute best five% of photoreceptors and are mainly focused within the fovea, in which their density decreases unexpectedly as they pass. On the other hand, Rods represent almost ninety 5% of photoreceptor cells and feature their most density within the retina's peripheral retina earlier than reducing towards the fovea, wherein they'll be absent.

It is likewise vital to be aware that the fovea performs a crucial characteristic in our functionality to observe and understand fast. Indeed, whilst we take a look at, we in particular use our fovea to recuperation our eyes on the phrases and sentences we check, which lets in us to have a study faster and better recognize what we've got a observe.

Therefore, looking after our fovea and retaining appropriate seen acuity is crucial to actually enjoy all of the advantages of pace reading. To try this, it is advocated to protect our eyes from the blue slight of video display units, to position on shades whilst we're uncovered to daylight mild, and to take regular breaks to relax our eyes at the same time as we look at or work on a laptop.

It is actual that the cones, which might be extra sensitive to information, contribute to a advanced visible acuity inside the center of our vision, just like the fovea, in comparison to the outer edge of our location of vision. However, this distinction in sensitivity is not the handiest reason for this superiority of visual acuity in the applicable location of the fovea.

Indeed, cones transmit visible information proper away to the mind. In assessment, statistics transmitted through rods is aggregated, i.E., information acquired thru numerous rods is averaged in advance than being transmitted to the brain with the resource of a unmarried ganglion cellular. This difference within the transmission of seen verbal exchange can also give an explanation for the prevalence of visible acuity in the fovea in evaluation to the outer edge.

This difference in an commercial enterprise organization influences the notion of micro-contrast. If one cone receives awesome moderate and its neighbor receives plenty less extreme slight, the brain will recognize a easy assessment amongst a band and a dark area. If, but, neighboring cones receive the same contrasting light, the thoughts will most effective see a grey vicinity, the forestall end result of the common between the moderate and darkish spots.

All this statistics about cones and rods appreciably influences how we study. Indeed, texts are made from lines, normally darkish on a light historic past, and being able to differentiate precisely a comparison amongst a moderate and a dark vicinity is crucial to understand the visible factors of the writing.

If the moderate imprint of a phrase touches the fovea, the cones will with out problems determine its records and transmit them with incredible fidelity to the thoughts. If, rather, the phrase touches the peripheral part of the retina (outdoor the fovea), it will be transmitted as a mean evaluation and could seem blurred to our thoughts. This is why our eyes make actions whilst we read, to maintain the phrase on the fovea and as a stop end result take a look at it efficaciously. The fovea is, therefore, the region in which most of the word recognition is completed.

Even if our visible acuity is advanced to the fovea, the records transmitted through the peripheral zones of our area of vision wants to be addressed genuinely. Numerous research have established that peripheral imaginative and prescient permits us to observe extra effectively.

For example, peripheral imaginative and prescient permits us to recognize powerful words, together with short phrases and acquainted terms, earlier than the fovea stops, permitting it to skip them to gain pace. Thus, peripheral vision is useful for reading, even though it does not allow visual acuity as acute because of the fact the fovea.

VI. Speed analyzing: 10 basics factor - keep away from commonplace errors

Read quicker at the same time as understanding

When reading velocity analyzing, it is crucial to understand the purpose of this approach. So what's the motive of tempo studying?

In fact, the purpose of pace analyzing is twofold. First, the reason of speed reading is to will permit you to check quicker. The faster you take a look at, the extra you can look at in less time. This will will let you maintain time to your each day existence, whether or not or no longer you're reading emails, articles, or books.

Second, pace analyzing targets to help you recognize what you're analyzing. If you take a look at quicker but want assist data what you are studying, you haven't obtained some thing. So pace reading permits you to study quicker even as better records what you are reading. This will will let you hold records greater efficaciously and use it greater productively.

You need to apprehend your starting component, as gaining knowledge of speedy studying begins offevolved offevolved with a vital assessment of your gift studying expertise. This assessment is crucial in identifying in which to pay attention your efforts and a way to boost up your increase.

A reading speed check is one of the first rate strategies to determine your analyzing tempo and comprehension degree. Numerous on line analyzing velocity exams are to be had, and they're capable of provide you with important records approximately your reading conduct and abilities. These checks are made to gauge how fast and thoroughly you read, and the outcomes may additionally display you what areas of your reading and comprehension need improvement.

You can greater successfully set wants to your pace analyzing improvement if you are aware of your starting degree. Having a particular motive in thoughts can help you live advocated and targeted even as you determine toward your purpose, whether or not to growth your analyzing velocity or beautify your comprehension.

It's moreover essential to display your improvement at the same time as working toward tempo studying. You can also see the practical outcomes of your hard paintings and resolution via way of manner of completing analyzing pace checks often and maintaining tune of your improvement. This can be inspiring and will inspire you to stay with your goal.

Knowing your area to begin is an crucial step in developing fast reading abilities. You may be higher organized to make massive development and get the consequences you want if you take the time to assess your present abilities and create attainable goals. Take a studying pace check to begin your route to becoming a quicker and greater effective reader!

It is likewise crucial to keep in mind the sort of text you are studying. If you observe in most times fiction, your analyzing tempo is probably special than analyzing articles or technical documents. So maintain in mind the form of textual content you have got a take a look at at the same time as comparing your reading pace.

Knowing your beginning diploma in pace reading will assist you progress and attain your studying desires. So don't hesitate to take a studying speed test and recollect the shape of text you study to decide your beginning degree in velocity studying. Then you could located into effect an movement plan to beautify your tempo and reading comprehension.

It is important to word that knowing your beginning diploma in tempo studying does now not imply you're restricted to that stage. Instead, it actually offers you a base to paintings from and permits you to determine your goals for improvement. So be recommended in case your analyzing pace is lower than you would love. With exercise and perseverance, you may enhance your pace and comprehension of speed analyzing.

Reading techniques and respiratory.

A precise approach is crucial for reading speedy and carefully information what you look at. But why is it so critical?

First of all, a fantastic reading approach permits you to have a observe faster. If you've got an effective analyzing technique, you may skim thru a textual content speedy and look at more phrases in lots much less time. This permit you to preserve time to your every day existence and revel in your analyzing more.

Second, a first-rate analyzing technique enables you apprehend what you are reading. If you have got got an useless studying method, you could want to absolutely apprehend what you are studying and lose track of the tale. With an effective analyzing method, you could better apprehend the textual content's standard which means and maintain the records more effectively.

Finally, an extraordinary analyzing technique allows you to take a look at extra effects and enjoyably. If you have got an vain studying method, you can get worn-out more rapid and grow to be discouraged.

With an effective analyzing method, you could have a observe more without problems and enjoyably, permitting you to get the most from your reading.

In precis, the importance of actual reading strategies want to be taken into consideration. It permits you to look at faster, to understand better what you're studying, and to check extra quite in reality and enjoyably. So in case you want to enhance your studying pace and comprehension, don't hesitate to work for your studying approach. It have to make all the distinction!

It is essential to have a look at that everybody has a completely particular studying approach, and there may be many tactics to enhance your analyzing approach. So, be recommended in case you want assist locating a way that works for you. Take the time to test and be conscious what works high-quality for you. By schooling super studying techniques and doing normal workout, you have to be capable of broaden an effective analyzing method with a purpose to will will let you have a look at faster and higher understand what you are reading.

To increase your reading speed, going for walks on your reading method is crucial. But what must you don't forget at the same time as walking for your studying method?

First, it's miles critical to artwork to your eye fixation. Your eyes need to skip over the text with out issue and at a regular speed. If your eyes stay on a letter or phrase for a fast time, it is able to sluggish down your studying pace. You can use a finger or stylus to conform with the textual content or a analyzing line to beautify your eye fixation.

Next, it's miles critical to artwork on key-phrase recognition. If you can brief apprehend key terms in a text, you may be able to recognize the overall which means of the text better and study faster. You can use memorization strategies to enhance your key-phrase recognition, which incorporates growing mental maps or writing summaries.

Finally, it's miles vital to artwork in your respiration while you have a examine. If you preserve your breath or breathe erratically, it could have an impact in your awareness and studying tempo. Try to breathe lightly and profoundly to decorate your reading speed.

The extraordinary forms of analyzing: pick out the right one for the scenario

There are numerous types of reading, and it is crucial to comprehend which ones to apply relying on the situation. But what are those unique types of analyzing, and the manner can you operate them effectively?

First, there can be linear analyzing. Linear studying involves studying a textual content sequentially, starting on the start and finishing at the prevent. This is the most commonplace form of analyzing and is proper whilst you want to apprehend the overall because of this of a textual content and preserve the data in detail.

Then there may be skimming. Skimming is analyzing a text speedy to get the gist and find essential information. It is helpful even as you need extra time to examine a whole textual content or while you need to discover essential statistics brief.

Finally, there is scanning. Scanning is the way of speedy skimming a textual content to discover specific facts. This is a valuable shape of studying whilst you need to discover a selected piece of statistics in a text short and also you fine have time to look at a part of the text.

There are numerous kinds of reading, and it's miles essential to select out the proper fashion for the state of affairs. Linear reading is good for information the general because of this of a text and retaining statistics in detail. Skimming is useful even as you need to discover crucial information in a textual content speedy. Scanning reading is beneficial whilst locating precise records in a text quick.

Therefore, selecting the right form of analyzing consistent with the situation is crucial to observe correctly. But why is it so critical to choose the proper kind of analyzing?

First, selecting the right form of reading will prevent time. If you use the right sort of analyzing, you'll be capable of read faster and discover the statistics you're seeking out greater without troubles. This allow you to keep time to your each day lifestyles and revel in your analyzing extra.

Second, selecting the right form of studying allows you higher recognize and maintain the facts. If you operate the ideal form of analyzing, you could want to certainly understand what you are reading or maintain the facts efficiently. By deciding on the proper shape of analyzing, you can higher recognize and preserve the information within the texts you have a study.

Finally, choosing the right shape of reading fabric permits you to have a take a look at greater effortlessly and enjoyably. If you operate the incorrect form of studying material, you may get worn-out extra fast and come to be discouraged. Choosing the suitable analyzing fabric lets in you to study greater genuinely and enjoyably, permitting you to get the maximum out of your analyzing.

Linear studying is the most commonplace shape of studying and is ideal for facts the general because of this of a textual content and retaining statistics in detail. However, there are a few situations wherein there are higher options than linear reading. But what are these situations, and why is linear reading not usually appropriate?

There are situations in which you need more time to look at a whole textual content. If you have a busy time desk and want to test an entire lot text, linear reading may additionally additionally need to be quicker and more inexperienced. In this example, it's far higher to use a quicker shape of analyzing, which incorporates skimming or scanning.

Then there are conditions in that you need to find out particular data in a textual content speedy. If you are seeking out a specific piece of statistics in a text and need greater time to observe the entire textual content, linear reading can also need to be faster and extra green. In this case, it's miles better to apply a quicker type of analyzing, such as scanning, which allows you to test a textual content to discover unique records speedy.

Finally, there are situations where you fine want to recognize or maintain some of the statistics of a textual content. If you are analyzing a textual content to get the gist and find key records, linear reading may be unnecessarily sluggish and sure. In this case, it's far better to use a quicker shape of studying, on the side of skimming, which allows you to short have a look at a textual content to recognize the gist and discover key facts.

So there are a few conditions with higher options than linear reading. If you don't have time to test an entire text, in case you want to locate a particular piece of data in a textual content fast, or if you don't want to understand or preserve all of the information of a text, it's pleasant to use a faster form of reading.

In summary, deciding on suitable reading cloth is essential for powerful analyzing. It saves time, enables you understand and keep statistics better, and makes studying more comfortable and thrilling. So, at the same time as you look at, recollect to pick out the right shape of studying for the situation to get the most benefit. By using those special styles of studying effectively, you have to higher understand and maintain the records within the texts you have got a observe.

Improve your records: visualization and memorization techniques.

Implementing visualization and memorization strategies is essential to beautify your records of what you examine. But how can you use the ones techniques efficaciously?

First, you can use the technique of creating highbrow maps. But what's mind mapping, and the way can it assist you higher apprehend and hold records?

Creating highbrow maps is the approach of graphically representing the facts in a textual content through diagrams or schematics. This permits you to visualize the enterprise of the facts and understand how all of the ideas are associated. For example, in case you are reading a textual content about the records of France, you may create a highbrow map representing the essential events inside the data of France and how they relate to each different.

By growing intellectual maps, you can better understand the data enterprise in a textual content and the way all the thoughts are related. This allows you to higher apprehend and maintain the facts in the texts you examine.

Next, you may use the approach of precis writing. Summary writing entails summarizing the data in a textual content concisely and as it ought to be. This allows you to apprehend better and undergo in mind the gist of what you have got examine. For instance, if you take a look at a text approximately brilliant sorts of clouds, you can write a summary of that textual content with the principle sorts of clouds and their developments.

When writing a precis, you ought in order to pick out out the most critical records and present it concisely and efficiently. This lets in you to understand better the essence of what you've got got look at and to keep in thoughts it greater without issue.

Finally, you can use the repetition approach. Repetition way repeating aloud or mentally the data you have got were given examine. This allows you to recovery the data in your memory and maintain it higher. For example, in case you test a textual content approximately the names of flowers, you may repeat the names of the flowers mentally or aloud to help you maintain in thoughts them.

By repeating the statistics you've got study, you restore the information on your reminiscence and are higher capable of preserve it.

The repetition technique includes repeating aloud or mentally the statistics you've got have a look at. This technique is easy and easy to put into effect however can be a whole lot much less effective than the "active maintain in thoughts" approach. By repeating the records you have got study, you aren't checking whether or not or not you have were given understood it, and you need to paintings on information the statistics.

On the opportunity hand, the energetic undergo in thoughts consists of answering questions or reciting the records you have got observe. This approach is extra effective than repetition because it permits you to test your information of the records and paintings for your comprehension. By answering questions or actively reciting the records you have got have a examine, you're forced to take into account it and relate it to what you recognize.

To use the "active take into account" approach in velocity analyzing, right right here are some steps to examine:

1. Select the most crucial statistics from the text you are studying. This allows you to aim the most applicable information and interest on it.

2. Formulate questions about the information you've got were given were given determined on. For instance, if you are reading a textual content about the information of France, you could ask questions like "When have become the French Republic proclaimed?", "Who come to be the primary president of the French Republic?"

3. Answer the questions you have got formulated. This allows you to actively recite the facts you have got study and check for records.

four. Repeat the exercise numerous times to recuperation the information on your memory. The greater you repeat the exercise, the extra you may be able to preserve the information completely.

Focus and distraction: stay centered on your reading

Have you ever located your self reading a text with out sincerely know-how its content material material? You might also have been distracted thru your mobile phone, paintings environment, or special out of doors factors. To better understand and preserve the information you are reading, it's far critical to interest on what you are reading and no longer be distracted through way of out of doors factors.

You can be used to reading whilst multitasking, this is at the same time as doing severa duties at the same time. For instance, you may read a text on the equal time as searching TV or paying attention to song. However, multitasking can be counterproductive, because it prevents you from focusing on what you are reading and higher information the statistics.

To keep away from being distracted through external factors, right here are some recommendations for enforcing:

1. Create a quiet and exquisite art work surroundings. If you are continuously distracted via noise or elements in your paintings environment, growing a non violent, best workspace to interest on what you are studying is important.

2. Unplug your telephone or positioned it on "do now not disturb" mode at the same time as you look at. This will will let you pay interest with out being interrupted thru notifications or calls.

3. Use a distraction-blocking software, which embody Freedom or Cold Turkey, to dam access to positive net websites or programs that can distract you even as you take a look at.

four. Take everyday breaks to loosen up and refocus. Taking time to loosen up and refocus allow you to pay attention better while you pass returned in your analyzing.

five. Make a issue listing and plan your studying time. If you want assist specializing in what you are studying, it may be beneficial to devise your analyzing time and prioritize the texts you want to examine. This will help you reputation on what's maximum vital and be targeted on more pressing obligations.Here's a manner you could use to popularity in five minutes:

1. Find a nice, quiet vicinity to sit down or lie down. Avoid sitting in a noisy or colorful region.

2. Close your eyes and take severa deep breaths. Try to loosen up and refocus in your breathing.

three. Do a small meditation exercise. You can recollect a non violent panorama or reputation on a mantra or a powerful phrase. This will help you loosen up and refocus.

4. Open your eyes and study an object in the distance. It may be a tree, a cloud, or every distinct item. Try to attention in this object for a few minutes.

five. Return on your present day analyzing or mission. Try to cognizance in your movements and not be distracted by means of way of outside elements.

6. By imposing this technique, you should be higher capable of attention and apprehend what you are studying or doing.

Speed reading: don't push too hard on the start

When you first begin the use of the velocity reading technique, it is tempting to need to look at as fast as possible to obtain better effects. However, it's far crucial to take a look at slowly inside the beginning, as this will be discouraging and feature an impact on your comprehension.

Reading too rapid can go away you needing to recognize all of the facts within the text and feeling aggravated. This can discourage you from continuing your pace studying exercise.

It is, therefore, important to start slowly and art work your manner up to improve your studying pace. By growing your analyzing tempo step by step, you will be better able to apprehend and maintain what you study.

Setting affordable goals and on the lookout for to benefit a immoderate studying velocity slowly is likewise crucial. Speed studying takes practice and staying power, and it's far regular no longer to acquire dramatic outcomes at the primary try.

Therefore, you shouldn't get discouraged and persevere for your pace reading exercising. By working toward often and setting less expensive desires, you will be capable of beautify your reading speed and gain better consequences sustainably.

Speed analyzing is definitely one device to enhance your comprehension and preserve in thoughts of what you have a observe. It is, consequently, critical to awareness on some thing apart from your studying pace and to be aware of other studying strategies, together with developing intellectual maps or writing summaries, which also can assist you better apprehend and hold what you test.

You ought to set reasonably-priced and feasible desires even as the usage of the rate analyzing technique. For instance, you can set a aim to growth your reading tempo by means of 10% every week or to examine a e-book of X pages in X hours.

These goals furthermore need to be unique and measurable, so that you can inspect your development and recognise in that you stand. For example, you could set a motive to look at a three hundred-internet page e-book in three hours and use a stopwatch to degree your reading time and make certain you're meeting your goal. Then repeat that reason in three months in a whole lot an awful lot much less time.

Set desires that encourage you to persevere on your tempo studying workout. For example, you could set a aim to have a look at a ebook out of your studying listing using the fee analyzing approach or to study a e-book for work or entertainment the use of speed reading.

Improve your studying comprehension and pace: observe aloud.

Reading aloud may be an powerful way to enhance your analyzing comprehension and speed. By studying aloud, you are compelled to recognition more on the text and take a look at more slowly, which allow you to higher apprehend what you're studying.

In addition, through studying aloud, you could pay interest the phrases and terms you are having problem with and live on them to better understand them. This may be especially useful in case you need assist knowledge powerful additives of the text or in case you come upon phrases you want to investigate.

Finally, reading aloud will let you boom your pronunciation and diction, that would benefit your commonplace communication.

It is essential to test that reading aloud is not a tempo reading approach however a complementary method that permit you to enhance your comprehension and reading tempo. Therefore, it's miles vital to permit yourself to study aloud and hold walking on precise elements of pace studying, which include eye fixation, key-word reputation, and breathing.

Also, it is critical not to examine aloud in a run of the mill or dull manner, as this could demotivate and discourage you from studying. Try to vary your intonation and rhythm to make your studying greater fun and appealing.

Finally, finding the right balance among reading aloud and silently is essential. Try to study aloud frequently, but handiest from time to time, so that you don't get used to it and maintain to growth your silent analyzing competencies.

Silent reading is analyzing for your head without saying the phrases out loud. Subvocalization, rather, consists of mentally saying the terms you look at in your head.

Silent reading is typically considered extra effective than subvocalization as it lets in you to have a look at quicker. Subvocalization can sluggish down your reading velocity because it calls in an effort to pronounce every phrase you take a look at mentally.

It is essential to note that subvocalization is a natural mechanism that allow you to apprehend and preserve in mind what you take a look at. However, it is viable to reduce subvocalization with the resource of running closer to silent studying and going for walks for your analyzing technique.

To lessen subvocalization and enhance your analyzing pace, there are numerous strategies you could attempt:

Use arms or markers to comply with the strains of textual content to avoid mentally announcing each phrase.

Use a voice reader, consisting of a text-to-speech software, as a manner to assist you to examine quicker at the same time as now not having to pronounce every phrase mentally.

Practice silent analyzing, this means that that analyzing on your head without announcing the terms out loud.

Work in your studying approach in favored, inclusive of eye fixation and key-phrase recognition.

It is vital to word that reducing subvocalization is tough to grasp and calls for education and workout. It is, therefore, critical to persevere and keep to art work in this hassle of velocity analyzing to look long-term results.

Take breaks for higher retention.

Taking ordinary breaks is crucial to keeping your attention and comprehension while you examine. It permits you to relaxation your eyes and mind and preserve what you look at higher.

It is normally endorsed which you take a wreck every 20-half-hour of analyzing, counting on your studying pace and fatigue diploma. During those breaks, you may near your eyes and lighten up for a couple of minutes or stroll and stretch to loosen up your muscle mass.

It is likewise vital to differ your interest in the course of your breaks. For example, you could do some workout, meditate, or chat with a pal or colleague. This will assist you live focused and maintain what you've got have a look at better.

In precis, regular breaks are crucial to preserve attention and reading comprehension. Don't hesitate to vary your sports activities at some point of those breaks to stay focused and hold what you have got got have a study better.

Sleep is also one of the crucial elements of reminiscence and analyzing. During sleep, our brains kind and shop the facts we've were given received in some unspecified time in the future of the day, which lets in us to preserve it better.

Studies show that sleep performs a important characteristic in consolidating lengthy-term reminiscence. During sleep, our brains evaluation facts discovered in some unspecified time in the future of the day and bolstered neural hyperlinks, allowing us to recall it higher.

Therefore, getting enough sleep is important to allow our brains to artwork effectively and maintain what we've were given look at or determined better. According to specialists, it is advocated to sleep amongst 7 and nine hours consistent with night to be healthy and healthful. I

Four texts to workout tempo analyzing

To improve your tempo analyzing abilties, four exercise texts will assist you expand your analyzing tempo at the identical time as retaining proper comprehension. Whether you're a amateur or need extra workout, the ones texts are suitable for all tiers and could provide a stimulating mission. Start with the number one textual content and artwork your manner as plenty due to the fact the remaining to peer your development and attain new analyzing velocity dreams. Remember to make the effort to recognize what you're analyzing, as that is the number one reason of tempo studying. Have an wonderful workout!

To calculate the studying speed of a textual content, you may use the following additives: Reading pace (phrases consistent with minute) = amount of terms/analyzing time (in mins)

For instance, in case you observe the primary 305-phrase textual content in 7 mins, your reading speed might be Reading speed (phrases constant with minute) = 305 phrases / 7 minutes = 40 3,fifty seven phrases constant with minute.

TEXT 1: 366 terms

Philosophers, scientists, and ordinary human beings have all been inquisitive about the assignment of time for a long term. We all have a finite quantity of it, however it is an with out end charming idea. Managing our time correctly is important due to the reality every 2nd is treasured and can not be retrieved after it has handed. The adage "time is coins" refers to this case, despite the fact that, in fact, time is significantly more valuable than cash. Time cannot be made up, however cash may be made, spent, or maybe out of place.

Using time manipulate techniques at the side of tempo analyzing is in reality one in every of them. One can study extra speedy the usage of eye motion and information-processing techniques even as nonetheless data what they're analyzing. People who need to take a look at content material cloth fabric fast and function busy schedules might also moreover discover this method mainly beneficial.

You can use a few techniques to hone your velocity-reading competencies. The first is through doing specific sports activities superior to decorate studying pace. For example, you could purpose to complete studying little texts in a predetermined quantity of time or test prolonged substances speedy via phrase skimming. There are one of a kind software program equipment for speed analyzing education that provide physical games and keep tabs for your progress.

Regular studying is the second one technique for developing pace studying. As you look at extra, you'll revel in extra cushty with the workout and be capable of pick out up reading pace more brief. Additionally, choosing books that interest you will assist you stay encouraged and focused.

It is critical to keep in mind that studying comprehension shouldn't be sacrificed for short studying. The technique is satisfactory beneficial in case you observe slowly and need help records the content fabric cloth. It is truly useful to observe slowly and thoroughly, and be ambitious and waft over some passages another time if you want to. You might also decorate your pace reading abilties and emerge as greater effective for your every day lifestyles with time, endurance, and workout.

In cease, time is a treasured aid that shouldn't be ignored. Striking a balance amongst pace and comprehension is critical at the same time as using pace studying as a technique for time control. You can beautify your velocity studying abilties and make the most of the little time we have were given in life thru running in the direction of frequently and exercise endurance.

TEXT 2: 293 phrases

Memory is an important cognitive function that allows us to shop and consider facts. It is break up into elements: quick-time period memory and extended-time period memory. Short-term reminiscence is sort of a buffer that permits us to in quick maintain information earlier than shifting it to long-time period memory. Long-time period memory is kind of a hard force that holds statistics completely.

Speed studying can be an powerful way to boost your reminiscence. By analyzing short, you pressure your mind to manner records quicker, that can decorate your capability to recollect. However, studying at an cheaper pace is crucial at the fee of comprehension. You want to recognize what you're studying to preserve in thoughts it correctly.

There are numerous strategies to beautify your reminiscence using tempo reading. The first is to study frequently. The extra you look at, the more your thoughts may be educated to machine and don't forget information quick. You also can check texts that interest you, as you may then be more advocated and targeted.

Another way to enhance your reminiscence is to check what you've got were given examine often. This can be finished with the resource of rereading the text, making evaluate playing cards, or discussing the content cloth with someone else. This let you recall and hold the data in the end.

Finally, searching after your intellectual and physical fitness is critical. A healthful eating regimen, everyday exercising, and specific pressure control can all help beautify your memory. Feel loose to take time to lighten up and unwind in order that your brain can function efficiently.

In precis, tempo studying can be an powerful way to enhance your memory so long as you don't neglect about comprehension and deal with your highbrow and physical fitness. With exercise and persistence, you need to be capable of develop your velocity analyzing abilities and support your reminiscence.

TEXT 3: 508 terms

I want to determine out wherein to start. I have become taken thru marvel. I didn't assume our courting to give up the way it did. We had been collectively for over years, and the whole thing regarded to be going nicely. We had our united statesand downs like every couple, but I became glad we have been purported to be together.

Then in the destiny, she informed me she needed to take time for herself. She said she didn't apprehend what she desired and needed time faraway from me to maintain in mind it. I come to be stuck off guard. I didn't count on that in any respect. I tried to persuade her to live, but she modified into enterprise. She said she wanted time and had to understand how long it'd take.

I become devastated. I didn't understand what to do. I attempted to expose her how hundreds I loved her and what sort of I desired her to stay, however she became determined to go away. I sooner or later popular her preference, even though it broke my coronary heart. I tried to give her area and understand her need for time, however it turn out to be tough. I couldn't save you considering her and questioning what have become occurring.

In the prevent, she in no way came decrease decrease again. She knowledgeable me that she had made up her thoughts and didn't need to be with me anymore. I turn out to be fully devastated. I couldn't accept as actual with that our relationship come to be over. I tried to influence her to exchange her mind, but she have end up decided. I in the long run conventional the reality and started out in search of to float on.

It come to be one of the worst tales of my existence. I will in no manner forget how I felt once I decided that the person I had shared a lot with now not favored to be with me. I'm despite the fact that looking for to determine out what occurred. We had our americaand downs like several couple, but I believed we'd get thru all our problems collectively. I end up stuck off guard with the useful resource of her desire to move away and had a hard time accepting it. I attempted to expose her how a first rate deal I cherished her and what form of I preferred her to stay, but she turn out to be business enterprise.

I went thru all kinds of emotions for the duration of this difficult time. I felt sadness, anger, sadness, and disbelief. I determined it hard to accept as real with that our relationship have emerge as over, and I spent plenty time seeking to determine out what had occurred. Eventually, I came to terms with fact and began out to try to pass on, even though it have grow to be tough.

I can't say I'm absolutely over that breakup. It's some thing if you want to stay with me forever. But I actually have found out a first-rate deal from this revel in and have grown as a person. I determined to be more potent and no longer permit my coronary coronary heart be broken on this manner in the future. I also observed out the importance of speakme brazenly and in fact in a relationship and now not being afraid to mention what I experience. This experience modified into painful, but I ended up reading precious education that allows you to serve me in the route of my life.

TEXT 4: 270 terms

The area expedition is one of the most ambitious traumatic situations humanity has ever confronted. Since man first set foot at the Moon in 1969, we've were given were given made infinite advances in location exploration. We have sent probes into the solar device, built area stations to house astronauts in orbit, or perhaps sent rovers to Mars.

But space exploration additionally brings many stressful conditions and dangers. Astronauts who skip on missions have to cope with extreme conditions, along with the vacuum of area, solar storms, and cosmic radiation. They also need to cope with intellectual stress and stress, as they will be regularly reduce off from the world for prolonged periods.

Despite those disturbing situations, area day trip stays an exciting and captivating region. It lets in us to discover new subjects about our planet and the universe spherical us. It moreover offers us new views on life and humanity's feasible opportunities.

Space tour is also a constantly evolving field. We recently released the number one crewed assignment to Mars and function many projects underway to find out different additives of the universe. We have additionally advanced new era, together with reusable rockets and self enough place vehicles, to make area missions extra stable and extra inexperienced.

In summary, region exploration is a charming and exciting location that allows us to discover new topics about our universe and planet. Despite the disturbing conditions and risks, we've had been given made many advances in region exploration and feature many obligations underway to maintain exploring the universe. We have additionally advanced new era to make area missions extra secure and extra green. Space day ride is an ever-evolving area, and I sit up for seeing what the future holds.

VII. Improve your reading tempo thru running on your method

It is crucial to emphasize that the ten elements mentioned above have clean theoretical rate and are critical to your mastering speed analyzing. They provide the foundation for constructing your mastery of this functionality.

However, it is also essential to workout greater advanced strategies as a manner to will let you accelerate your analyzing whilst maintaining a excessive level of comprehension. Although this listing isn't always exhaustive, I will gift proper here people who have helped me for my part, in addition to the ones who have showed to be powerful for the humans I truly have had the possibility to accompany in their improvement in pace reading.

Hover and experiment

Scanning is a quick-reading method that allows you to rapid system a massive amount of data in a quick time. This approach consists of brief skimming a textual content to get a top level view, then scanning the most critical records for a deeper facts.

Scanning is beneficial for quick studying prolonged, complex texts, which incorporates research articles or technical books. It lets in you to technique information fast to apprehend the text's essence and orient your self indoors it.

Using the Hover and Scan approach, you may enhance your analyzing speed and comprehension of text. This approach permit you to approach data better and make higher decisions quicker. If you need to decorate your studying pace and information of texts, the Hover and Scan method is one to attempt.

The rapid flyover

Skimming is a quick analyzing approach that allows you to speedy procedure a big quantity of records in a brief period. This approach will will let you get an outline of a textual content and to orient your self in it. It is beneficial whilst you want to understand the gist of a text while now not having to look at each word.

There are severa soaring techniques you can use depending in your analyzing goals. Here are a few examples of hovering strategies:

The take a look at-aloud technique: This method includes reading aloud, eliminating unnecessary phrases, and emphasizing key phrases. It lets in you to procedure information and orient your self inside the textual content fast.

The diagonal skimming technique: This approach includes quick reading the pinnacle lines from left to proper, then the bottom lines from proper to left, and so on. It permits you to technique facts and orient your self inside the text brief.

Skimming with the useful resource of rule: This technique includes brief studying each line via following a rule (as an example, thru following a finger or a stylus) and putting off vain terms. It allows you to way records and orient yourself inside the text quick.

Using the hover method, you can short way facts and orient yourself in a text. Feel unfastened to try splendid hovering strategies to locate the simplest that works extremely good for you.

The take a look at

Speed scanning is a studying method that objectives to boom reading velocity at the identical time as retaining unique comprehension. It includes "searching" for important statistics in a text the use of a tempo analyzing technique.

To use this method, knowledge what you're seeking out is crucial in advance than you start reading. This lets in you to consciousness on critical records to acquire that aim. It is also vital to familiarize yourself with the content material material of the text earlier than you begin studying to understand wherein to look for important data.

Several scanning techniques for pace studying, inclusive of "slit" or "location" studying. Slit" analyzing entails the use of the eyes to "test" the textual content using giant horizontal slits overlaying numerous traces concurrently. Zone studying uses the eyes extra vertically, analyzing organizations of terms as adverse to complete strains.

It is critical to have a take a look at that pace scanning isn't always appropriate for all types of textual content. It is beneficial for reading informational or fictional documents but can be an entire lot much less amazing for studying technical or scientific papers that require hobby to detail.

Here are 5 steps to installation a tempo experiment:

1. Determine what you're searching out: Before you start reading, it's miles essential to apprehend what you're looking for inside the textual content. This may be a elegant concept, a selected idea, or statistics. This will can help you attention on essential facts to attain your cause.

2. Familiarize your self with the text: Before you start analyzing, skim and familiarize yourself with its contents. Look at the headings, subheadings, and key terms to apprehend what is in each segment. This will assist you recognize where to look for essential records.

three. Choose a velocity analyzing approach: There are numerous pace analyzing techniques, together with "slit" or "area" reading. Choose the best that fits you super and allows you to have a look at speedy at the same time as records the content material of the text.

four. Start reading: Once you have got were given determined what you're searching out and characteristic decided on a pace studying method, start studying the textual content. Use your pace analyzing method to "hunt" for crucial information and discover new mind.

five. Take notes: As you read, take notes on what you have got observe. This will assist you higher recognize and endure in mind the content of the text. You also can use those notes to take a look at later.

In summary:

Start with a brief skim of the textual content to get a pinnacle stage view and orient yourself to the text. You can use skimming strategies which encompass studying diagonally or reading aloud to approach statistics short.

Identify the maximum important records and awareness on it even as scanning. You can use scanning strategies which includes twin view or rule reading to system this information extra thoroughly.

Take notes at some stage inside the test that will help you keep facts higher. You can use word-taking techniques such as mind mapping or concept mapping to arrange your thoughts truely and concisely.

Practice the Hover and Scan method frequently to improve your studying tempo and comprehension of text. Practice is essential to decorate your studying velocity and capability to technique statistics quick. Take the time to often look at and workout the Hover and Scan method to beautify reading velocity and comprehension.

Adapt your skimming and scanning approach in step with your studying goal. If you want to recognize the entire textual content, you could want to spend greater time scanning the facts. If you are looking for a pinnacle stage view of the text, you can want to spend a bargain less time scanning the facts.

Improve velocity analyzing

Improving linear reading in tempo reading may be very useful for severa reasons.

First of all, linear analyzing in pace studying can assist enhance comprehension of the text. When you study linearly, you comply with the glide of the textual content constantly, which permits you to apprehend the drift of thoughts and maintain the content material of the text higher.

Second, linear pace analyzing may be useful for immediate finding precise facts in a textual content. When you observe linearly, you may use pace analyzing techniques to "hunt" for vital information and find out new thoughts. This lets in you to speedy discover the statistics you are looking for without going thru the whole text.

Finally, linear analyzing in tempo studying can be beneficial to maintain higher and use the records you have had been given take a look at. When you examine linearly, you could take notes and make summaries that will help you better understand and do not forget the content material of the textual content. You can also use these notes to take a look at later and follow your determined out statistics.

Find fixing elements

The fixation factors in tempo analyzing are factors on which the eyes rest in the end of reading. They play an essential role in studying velocity and text comprehension.

Several factors may want to have an effect on the fixation factors in speedy reading. First, the studying method used can have an impact on fixation factors. For instance, the "slit" analyzing method involves the use of huge horizontal slits to cowl numerous traces concurrently, that might bring about broader fixation factors. In evaluation, the "vicinity" studying method makes use of more minor fixation factors to observe companies of terms in desire to entire strains.

Second, the content material fabric of the textual content will have an effect at the fixation factors. For example, if the textual content is dense and complicated, the fixation factors can be smaller to allow for better information.

Finally, the reader's familiarity with the text will have an impact on fixation elements. If the reader is familiar with the content material material cloth of the text, he may have more fantastic fixation elements due to the reality he already has an superb know-how of the statistics. On the alternative hand, if the reader isn't familiar with the textual content content material, they may have greater minor fixation factors to apprehend the statistics better.

It is critical to be conscious that fixation points in pace analyzing can variety relying on the man or woman and the situation. No "perfect" fixation element length will artwork for all readers in all conditions.

However, by means of the usage of way of jogging for your reading method and thinking of the content material and familiarity degree of the text, you can alter your fixation factors to decorate your studying pace and comprehension.

It is also difficult to offer a very particular huge shape of fixation factors on common because of the reality they might variety relying on numerous elements, which include the reading technique used, the content material fabric of the textual content, and the reader's degree of familiarity with the text.

It is anticipated that the quantity of fixation factors in rapid analyzing can range from 10 to 20 in step with minute. However, this huge variety can be better or decrease relying on the state of affairs. For example, if you are studying dense, complicated text, you may need greater fixation factors to apprehend the records higher. On the opportunity hand, in case you are acquainted with the content material fabric of the text, you could need fewer fixation points because of the reality you have already got a top notch know-how of the information.

The type of fixation elements is not continually a hallmark of analyzing pleasant. Some readers might also have a better massive sort of fixation elements but better text comprehension, at the same time as others may also have a lower form of fixation factors however worse comprehension. The important trouble is to discover a analyzing approach that works for you and allows you to observe efficaciously and understand the content of the text.

Expand the sector of vision.

When you examine, your visual field is the location of your vision that covers the text you're analyzing. The narrower your challenge of vision, the extra time you want to test the text, and the much more likely you'll make errors or pass over critical data. By widening your region of imaginative and prescient, you may cowl greater phrases at a time and decorate your studying tempo at the identical time as keeping a terrific expertise of the text.

It is essential to be conscious that growing the visual view in velocity analyzing takes exercising and workout. You can start with smooth sporting events to help you come to be familiar with the method and increase your field of vision. With exercise, you have to have the ability to seriously widen your field of imaginative and prescient and decorate your analyzing pace while retaining a tremendous information of the textual content.

Here are four sports activities that will let you growth your field of regard in pace analyzing:

Slot" exercise: This exercise involves analyzing strains of terms using big horizontal slots. To begin, location your index finger on the first line of phrases and flow into it horizontally to cover severa words concurrently. Drag your index finger to the following line and repeat until you've protected the whole text. You can adjust the width of the slot to suit your consolation diploma and analyzing pace.

Zone" exercising: This workout consists of analyzing corporations of phrases the usage of more minor fixation elements. To begin, region your index finger on the number one organization of phrases and go with the flow it from left to proper to cover every phrase in my view. Drag your index finger to the subsequent agency of terms and repeat till you've blanketed the entire textual content. You can modify the scale of the phrase corporations to fit your consolation diploma and analyzing pace.

"Vertical Slots" exercising: this workout consists of reading columns of terms the use of huge vertical slots. To start, area your index finger at the primary column of phrases and float it vertically to cover several terms simultaneously. Drag your index finger to the following column and repeat till you've covered all of the textual content. You can regulate the width of the slot to suit your consolation stage and reading tempo.

Scanning" exercise: This exercising consists of rapid scanning the textual content the use of a single difficulty of fixation. To start, location your index finger on the primary line of words and float it horizontally to cover every phrase for my part. Drag your index finger to the subsequent line and repeat till you have got were given got blanketed the entire textual content. You can modify the movement tempo to suit your consolation stage and reading tempo.

Train your eyes

It is important to understand how your eye movements artwork whilst reading. Your eyes skip inconsistently, stopping on some phrases and ignoring others. If you could lessen the kind of actions you are making in line with line, you may be able to have a observe an lousy lot quicker. However, it is probably terrific when you have been careful due to the truth there can be a limit to the amount of terms you may recognize at one time.

According to three research, you can have a look at 8 letters on the right of your eye characteristic but most effective 4 at the left, which is ready to a few terms every time. In addition, you could have a study amongst nine and fifteen spaces at the right, however you can't have a examine them. Regular readers additionally do not way words on specific lines.

To exercise, try skipping traces while information what you're analyzing. This have to be highly easy when you get the hang of it.

To improve your analyzing tempo, it is essential to exercising lowering the style of eye moves. This is because of the reality your mind normally determines where to direct your eyes primarily based mostly on the duration or familiarity of the following phrase. If you could get your eyes used to transport appropriately during the web web page, you may be capable of study faster.

Here's a easy workout to help you workout:

Place your bookmark on a line of text.

Draw an X at the bookmark, really above the primary phrase.

Draw each other X on the equal line, placing it 3 terms away for clean comprehension, five phrases out for intermediate-diploma textual content, and seven phrases away for greater tough text.

Continue to draw X's spaced out within the equal manner until the stop of the road.

Read rapid with the useful resource of the use of sliding the bookmark down, focusing your eyes handiest under each X.

This workout will will assist you to teach yourself to lessen your eye actions and attention on specific phrases, that lets in you to help you read faster even as preserving proper comprehension.

One of the matters that could slow down your studying pace the most are regressions and backspaces. Indeed, the ones moves can save time, so it is critical to avoid them to beautify your analyzing pace.

But what exactly is regression? It is the act of rereading terms or sentences you've got already have a look at. This normally happens at the same time as you observed you continue to want to maintain or apprehend what you've really look at. However, it's miles vital to have a look at that your mind has most in all likelihood retained the data, even if you feel in any other case.

To get rid of regressions, it's far crucial to exercise now not going decrease back even in case you suppose you've got however to recognize the textual content. Continue analyzing and permit your eyes go with the flow in advance. Here's an exercise that will help you workout:

1. Take a medium-stage text and region your bookmark at the number one line.

2. Begin studying via letting your eyes go along with the float over every line without looking once more.

3. If you want assist expertise a word or sentence, don't pass once more and re-observe it. Just preserve analyzing and allow your mind combine the records as you go.

4. Repeat this exercising until you can look at the textual content with out returning.

You can check an lousy lot quicker with the aid of education eliminating regressions and backtracking while maintaining comprehension.

Trusting your thoughts

It is crucial to consider your thoughts for comprehension in pace reading. Our brains can manner big portions of data rapid and efficaciously, which allows us to have a look at rapid on the same time as preserving a first-rate information of the text.

Relaxing and focusing at the textual content is vital to accept as actual together with your brain in tempo analyzing. By the use of a tempo reading approach that fits your analyzing style and taking the time to get yourself up to speed with the content material cloth of the textual content in advance than you start reading, you may help your mind higher understand the records.

It is also important now not to fear if you don't apprehend all the statistics proper away. Our brains can memorize and manner massive quantities of records, even though we don't recognize it right now.

It is also vital to test and memorize the facts you look at. By repeating the content fabric of the text aloud or writing a precis, you could assist your thoughts better do not forget the facts and hold it within the long time.

In precis, trusting your mind in pace studying is essential for suitable sufficient text comprehension. By the use of a pace analyzing technique appropriate on your reading style, taking the time to make yourself familiar with the content cloth of the textual content, and reviewing and memorizing the facts have a observe, you could assist your thoughts better apprehend and hold the information observe brief and successfully.

Note-taking approach

Taking notes whilst pace studying may be very helpful in improving comprehension and retention of the textual content you look at. Taking notes for the duration of the studying can help your thoughts higher device and preserve the data in the long term.

There are severa methods to take notes in pace reading, collectively with conventional word-taking, the Cornell technique, and word-taking the usage of diagrams and charts. Each method has blessings and drawbacks, and it's far essential to discover the only that great suits your analyzing fashion and dreams.

Rapid studying be aware-taking also can be beneficial to help you make clear your thoughts and shape your thinking. By summarizing the textual content you observe and rephrasing it on your very own way, you may better apprehend the content material and apply it to your lifestyles or art work.

Many techniques of have a look at-taking are taken into consideration the incredible in step with medical studies. According to investigate, the most suitable examine-taking technique depends on severa elements, along with the character's analyzing fashion, the text's complexity, and the studying's context.

However, a few studies have shown that look at-taking the use of diagrams and charts may be extra powerful for some humans as it permits them to visualise requirements greater truely and higher understand the form of the textual content. Other studies have tested that be aware-taking using the Cornell approach, which incorporates dividing the web page into columns and taking notes the usage of short sentences and key phrases, can be extra powerful for a few humans as it lets in to shape the records greater absolutely.

It is crucial to examine that the first rate word-taking technique is based upon on your picks and studying style. It can be beneficial to check one in every of a kind take a look at-taking techniques and discover the best that amazing fits your analyzing style and needs.

It is likewise important to word that pace-reading word-taking is best important for some and might not be the remarkable method for all text types. According to 3 research, have a look at-taking can also even lessen attention and comprehension for a few humans.

Therefore, locating an technique that fits your studying style and goals is essential. If you are taking notes in pace studying, it's essential to consciousness simplest a chunk on taking notes and make sure you apprehend the textual content in advance than moving immediately to the subsequent web page.

VIII. Optimize your studying speed steady with the medium: paper or digital

Speed analyzing is an essential knowledge that may be advanced and advanced, irrespective of the medium used. But how do you pick out out amongst studying on paper and virtual media?

According to research, studying on paper can be greater interesting for some readers because it lets in them to detach from the screen and awareness better on the text. It additionally can be less complicated for a few readers because it will allow them to manipulate their analyzing speed higher and not be distracted via notifications or outside hyperlinks. According to three studies, analyzing on paper may even assist with better comprehension and memorization of textual content, mainly for long or complex texts.

Therefore, reading on paper can be maximum green for some files requiring masses hobby and information. For example, in case you want to take a look at expert or educational documents, alongside aspect reviews, research articles, manuals, or textbooks, analyzing on paper let you higher recognize and consider the content material cloth cloth. Reading on paper is likewise most desirable in case you have to put together for checks or tests, as it allows you higher recognize and don't forget the cloth.

However, analyzing on virtual media may be extra available for some readers because it permits clean get entry to to greater information thru outside links. It can also be simpler for a few readers because it will allow them to control their studying tempo and spotlight or mark critical passages.

Therefore, digital analyzing is greatest for some materials requiring plenty practice and short comprehension. For instance, digital studying might be maximum green if you examine statistics or articles on-line as it let you examine fast and get proper of get right of entry to to more facts successfully. Digital analyzing is likewise final if you need to fast apprehend a big amount of facts, which includes emails or commercial corporation files.

www.ingramcontent.com/pod-product-compliance
Lightning Source LLC
Chambersburg PA
CBHW071447080526
44587CB00014B/2020